A FOUR WAY FORAY

FOR

FOUR WINDS

BY

W.H. Matlock III

xulon PRESS

A Four Way Foray For Four Winds
by W.H. Matlock III

Printed in the United States of America

ISBN 978-1-60791-350-4

www.xulonpress.com

Dear Richard,

First of all, tell your wife she didn't get her "props" because she looks so young. I had to call Chris and ask her if that was Shirley.

Secondly, the war is not against flesh and blood but against "principalities and powers". That translates into demonic principles and authorities who are the authors of those principles - this book is aimed at them. It's not what most folks call enjoyable reading.

Check out page 54. That will tell you where its coming from. Even under the circumstances, it was good to see you all.

Bill

To Richard

Was - brother in law
Is - brother in Christ

Bill Matlock

CONTENTS

PREFACE

The cover of this book is a copy of a house painter's first artistic effort on canvas. The title of the work is Thought Symbol. The painter considers his work to be a symbolic representation of totality. After years of scrutiny, this writer, admittedly not an authority, has not been able to find a single reason to disagree.

The Bible is this writer's template. Questions like: Does the Bible say that Jesus said "I am the door" were asked. Then: Is a door represented in the painting? The answer to both questions is yes. After a page of such questions and their affirmative answers, it was decided by this writer to leave further testing to theologians.

On the mundane level, questions like: Are there 12 hours in a day and 12 hours in a night? were asked. Then: Is that separation of day and night accounted for in the painting? Again, there were a goodly number of affirmative answers. In addition to those answers, it was noticed that the painting effortlessly squares the circle.

The physical eye sees only a tetragon of different shaded bands within bands. The eye of discernment discloses a 24 hour orbit of the earth around the sun. The bands within bands represent the hours in a day and a night. In effect, the bands translate into wheels within one orbital wheel. To look at the cover on this book is to see that the circle has been squared.

That tetragon can also be viewed as a pyramid without its headstone. From inside, standing on the pyramid's floor, its door is overhead. From outside and above the pyramid, the open door is down below. That optical illusion has no more to do with the occult than the sign of the cross. It's not even esoteric. It is a straight forward expression of mathematical functions embedded in reality.

By the way, the poems at the end of this book and the painting on its cover are, figuratively speaking, bookends. Though they were done in different decades, and without an iota of collusion, both the poems and the painting have to do with the same reality. The painting is a formalized graphic representation of totality. The poems are the base for a proliferating totality.

The painting is of squared bands of shades of gray that are also wheels within wheels. The band of poems are a bevy of flying wheels within wheels. They are also a string of pearls that either as a glow, a halo, or both, complement the beauty of the square of bands. Even as the painting squares the circle, the poems circle that square.

OPEN LETTER TO WHOSOEVER

Dear Whosoever:

Since the cosmos is the aftermath of creation, the Bible is the only math book in the world. When the word "science" is correctly defined, logic demands that it be viewed as a tertiary adjunct of omniscience, just as logic itself must be etymologically viewed as the property of the Logos. When "Christian science" is seen as a redundancy – because the Holy Spirit and the scientific method (righteousness) are essentially synonymous terms – the existence of God no longer needs to be considered a matter of faith because the Creator must, of necessity, be seen as <u>the</u> quintessential scientific fact.

If the existence of words is a scientific fact, questioning creation is proof of creation because the questions presuppose the language (Son of man) that presupposes the Word (the only begotten Son of God) that is the Creator.

It is impossible for anyone (aliens included) to even attempt to refute those facts without availing himself of the word. The word, which is the only (and ideal) vehicle of cerebration and verbal communication, is as misunderstood as the "simple" cell used to be. Every word, in any language, is an encapsulation of truth, reality, order, and light, — and is therefore an ethereal atom analogous to the one that is the building block of matter. That foundational fact, harder than any diamond, is an undeniable absolute. A sentence can lie. A word can't.

"In the beginning was the Word..." is more than just a scriptural verse. It is a cosmic law that, unlike the law of gravity, cannot be superceded by the law of aerodynamics, or any other law. Nothing can break that law, and nothing, ethereal or material, is exempt from it. In essence, the DNA molecule is itself a very, very, very, long word.

Anyone wishing to challenge those assertions has no choice but to avail himself of language to do so. In effect, the word in flesh (DNA) must avail itself of the ethereal word in order to express its disbelief in the sovereignty of the word. By doing so, that disgruntled body of flesh becomes living proof that the cosmic scheme of things is such that the sovereignty of the word is unchallengeable. For as long as that body remains in the flesh, that would-be challenger will face a closed loop that is not ever going to be open to question ...not without words.

It is therefore counterproductive for experts in apologetics to continue to labor so mightily in defense of the faith. To defend (as faith) that which is a provable scientific fact is to fall into a pseudoscientific trap. That trap is rendered useless by going on offense and attacking foolishness with a heavy dose of reality. Necessarily, that dosage will also include equal measures of truth, order, and light. The only things left for reality to attack are the lies and disorders that result in an absence of light.

Who can successfully deny that, in the cosmic scheme of things, the existence of the universe presupposes the omniscience from which it had to proceed? By definition, omniscience, of course, is all answer.

Any quest for an answer presupposes a departure from that omniscience. By strict adherence to the scientific method, a quest, if it is logical, will eventually return to omniscience. The course of the journey is from that fount of possibility, through being at a loss, to the arrival at the answer that is finally found to be a possibility. In that logical circuit, just as shadowy paradox is resolved in shadowless equinox, science is resolved in omniscience.

The failure to adhere to the scientific method results in the shortcomings and disorders of psuedoscience. It is a bare bones reality that God, omniscience, and science, are inextricable, one from the other. Psuedoscience, as ruthless as its agenda may be, is rootless.

The weapon most used by rootless, offensive, cultural warriors is the linguistic one employed to enshroud that reality in semantical clouds. That strategy is fatally flawed for the simple reason that there is no way to alter the fact that words are seminal in the formation of those clouds. Once access to the source of those seminal-antics is denied by the introduction of reality into the linguistic loop, the clouds dissipate. With their clearing, it becomes obvious to any scientific investigation that the answers in Genesis are as immutable as they are inalterable. No argument to the contrary can even begin without confirming the fact that "In the beginning was the Word…" is an unbreakable cosmic law.

DECLARATION OF DEPENDENCE

Since Genesis opens its curtain with the act of creation, it is not surprising that the Word would be the Star of stars at center stage. The eternal Word (IHVH) is the sign of the Designer of the word which is the building block of language. That ethereal vehicle is the perfect (and only) means of expressing ideas. Because the idea of there being such a vehicle is above and beyond the entropic principle which nature is subject to, by definition, both the idea of the vehicle and the vehicle itself, must, of necessity, be supernatural entities. The pairing of thought and symbol is a phenomenon of coded representation that is as inalterable as it is immutable.

Language may change, but the idea of there being a language to undergo change is also as inalterable as it is immutable. Moreover, it is an empirical reality that the ethereal vehicle, being inalterably unique, has to be the universal singularity which is the cosmic ideal as well. So, it stands to reason that the Logos (from which logic must proceed, and to which logical ideas must return) has to be the singularity that is ideal; and therefore has to be the Star that is the light of the world.

Light, knowledge, and science, are three words that are also synonymous terms. It goes without saying that, to be a word, they have to be paired with meaning. It doesn't take a lot of pondering to figure out why the dynamics involved in the formation of a word presuppose that the intrinsic integrity of that cosmic ideal will be intact. Essentially, it is agreement by two or more on the arrangement of mutually understood elemental symbols for the meaning that is being symbolized. If that vehicle conveys understanding, its integrity is innate. Unless there has been tampering, a single word cannot lie. Even when there is evidence of tampering, the lie will be spring loaded. It is ever at the ready to "out" itself.

The upshot is that when the word "science" is stripped of its pseudoscientific accretions it becomes glaringly obvious that science is a tertiary adjunct of omniscience. In that light, science and knowledge once again become synonymous terms. Thus, despite the best efforts of those who would stage-manage the scientific method by redefining terms, there is no question about any ultimate issue whose answer is not to be found in Genesis.

Once the sovereignty of the cosmic ideal's omniscience is comprehended, it becomes obvious that its existence presupposes both omnipresence and omnipotence. Scientifically sound experimentation will prove, quickly, that they are inextricably linked – each to both of the others. So, any idea attempting to oppose that sovereignty finds itself locked into a position where the more it argues its case the more it reduces its argument to absurdity – because it must avail itself of the vehicle whose singular stature it is arguing against. It is a cosmic reality that there is no way to oppose the sovereignty of the cosmic ideal without simultaneously affirming the sovereignty of the cosmic ideal. Any opposing idea relegates itself into having to occupy a position in the cosmic cul-de-sac.

The army of Post Modern intellects imagines that they are engaged in destroying the foundations of the protecting walls surrounding the answers in Genesis. In their blindness, those troops are unable to see that there is no idea that does not owe its existence to the self-authenticating cosmic ideal. One indication that such blindness abounds in their ranks is that time is viewed by them as an entity that can be given credit for healing wounds. Actually, the very best that time can do is to be a measure of how long it takes a wound to heal.

They also have no qualms about entertaining the absurd notion that time is a medium which a machine might be able to traverse. How they manage to avoid seeing that time is no more, and no less, than the abstract tool of measure extrapolated from the perfection of orbital speed would be a mystery were it not for the answer (found in Genesis) to the question of how such blindness could occur. It is far more logical to theorize that instantaneous apparitions are able to bypass time because of some sort of relationship between omnipresence and the present than it is to speculate about how a three dimensional machine can manage to travel in a dimensionless abstraction from the speed of orbital motion. Even though time may be the most important tool of measure in the third dimension, it is not itself a dimension.

At the same time that Post Modern blindness casts aspersions on the idea of there being any such thing as perfection, it views the array of digits (1-9) as being just about as close to perfection as it is possible to get. The truth of the matter is, since the cosmos is an adjunct of the universe, that there is a taxonomical gap between the 1 and the 2 so wide that a blinded carnal mind cannot help but be boggled at the suggestion that such a gap could even be possible.

Conventional thinking views the 1 as a number. It is not. Actually, the 1 is an extender of oneness throughout the cosmos. Everything, including the zero, has to be 1 of whatever it happens to be. At first glance, the problem may appear to be due to an inadvertent equivocation that resulted in the presentation of a false dichotomy. Or it may appear to be purely a matter of semantics. But, under higher mental magnification, it may be seen that the problem is a matter of the misrepresentation of the nature of numerical reality.

The 2 is the first digit that is capable of numbing a count. The 2 is frozen so solid that it can never be any more, or any less, than what it is. What is true of that number is true of every other number, no matter how large that number happens to be. While the 1 is a designator of things, numbers are abstract enumerators of the things that have been designated. The 1 extends. Numbers numb.

It must be acknowledged that arithmetical calculations will bear out the conventional view that there is no categorical difference between the 1 and the other digits – but only up to a point. Upon entrance into the realm of theoretical physics, semantics can have an influence on logic. Semantics give infinity credit for being open ended. That idea is a departure from reality.

While there is always room in the inn for at least one more in infinity; in reality, whenever that last one is counted or accounted for, infinity finds itself face to face with the omnipresence of the 1. Theory allows infinity to continue going on forever into what is considered to be nothingness. Logic demands that it stop and give up its claim to be infinite. The reality is that it is the 1 that is infinite.

Obviously, it is possible for numbers to appear to be saying one thing while logic definitely says another. A theorist who is not aware of that fact is in danger of falling into the trap of thinking he can draw a straight line with a bent ruler. In addition to that, the failure to take the nature of time, and the existence of the taxonomical gap, into account could possibly result in an arithmetically elegant, exquisitely constructed, flawless, formula that is a distortion of reality. The theory of relativity may manifestly be a three-dimensional fact, but as far as dimensionless reality is concerned, it is a nonevent.

It is inconceivable how it could be possible for there to be either warps in time, or time travel. When time is properly defined and correctly understood, the reason why it is inconceivable becomes obvious. Since time is a measure extrapolated from orbital motion that has been replicated in a calibrated mechanism, a warp in time would have to be the logical equivalent of there being a warp in the speed of orbital motion. The warp in that kind of reasoning readily transfers into a warp in logic. Just as the warp in logic disallows the idea of there being a warp in time (because the concept is illogical), so does the idea of time travel spontaneously abort because that which cannot be conceived cannot be. Perfection is an attribute of God. Time is an invention of man. It is the clock that has to be corrected.

It is conceivable that there may be curves, and therefore black holes, in space. It is also conceivable, if numbers and not observation are used to determine their existence, that there may not be. It might be that they and/or the nature of their characteristics are reflections of the unaccounted for warp in numbers.

It is common knowledge that when 10 is divided by 3, and that result is squared, the net result is a recurring (but not infinite) string of 9's. Imputation is required to get back to the original 10. The question of what happened to the missing tenth of a number (which would be a number) is unanswered. But it is not unanswerable. The imputation is of the logic that reflects the reality that, ultimately, the unifying field is an omnipresence that is only theoretically divisible. In reality, what is thought to be division is merely an extension of oneness.

It is also common knowledge that a living cell was once thought to be a simple gelatinous clot. The point is that it is risky to say what is, or is not, especially in the astrophysical theoretical realm, until more work is done on the numerical genome. But even after all that work is done, one thing is for sure – there will be no time travel.

The fact that the present is locked into an everlasting state of change means that it is relative to both the past and the future. It is also relative to the eternal now which is impervious to any kind of change. Since that ethereal anchor is above and beyond relativity, even though the present and the now are face to face, they face each other from across a taxonomical abyss. Theorists who are unaware of the taxonomical gap between the digits 1 and 2 will almost certainly be unaware of the gaping chasm between the present and the now. Even if they were to see that there is a difference between them, it would appear to those theorists that the present and the now are "separate but equal" parallel realities. But the present is not a reality at all.

Neither is it an illusion. It is a very real instance of motion being abstracted from earth's orbit around the sun and being theoretically frozen for the instant it takes to realize it was already a part of the past before it could be fully realized. The present is an enormously useful concept, but its usefulness is confined to the third dimension. Essentially, it is an artificial construct with no reality of its own. The best it can possibly attain to be is the shadow of a memory.

On the other hand, the now has always been the reality that it now is, and always will be. Though the now pervades the relativity of the present, relativity is barred from entering the timelessness of now. Put another way, the eternal realm permeates the third dimension, but no three dimensional object can enter that realm – not as a three dimensional object. No matter what the numbers say, think tank harems fantasizing about time machines are engaged in the enterprise of wasting time for fun and profit. After all, it is not the 32 degrees that turns water into ice… it's the cold weather. If there can be time travel, there can be degree travel.

On their best day, numbers are but a shadow of the omniscience of the reality symbolized by the digit 1. Any idea about the superiority of numbers is as inverted as the prevailing ideas about the origins of science. The alphabet can spell out any number (quintillion), but no amount of numbers can spell a single word. The answer to any questions about how those ideas got turned upside down can be found by reverse engineering them all the way back to the snake that slithered out on the limb of that tree in the garden of Eden. Put another way, the answer is in Genesis.

Thus, the species of blindness that would find it extremely difficult to comprehend how it is that numbers can numb and letters (alpha thru omega) can let, imagines that it is experiencing great success in marginalizing fools trumpeting the veracity of the answers in Genesis. It sees itself as the liberating army marching around outside the walls of a myth whose fate will be identical to that of Icarus. It imagines that the intellectual heat it has brought to bear is melting the wax fastening those wings on Icarus' back.

However, by strictly adhering to the logic intrinsic in the scientific method (whose fountainhead is the Logos), the only logical conclusion that can be drawn is that a species of intellects, which has yet to define the time it imagines can be a father, cannot know what time it is. It is the height of understatement to say that army will be shocked at the sound of the trumpet that causes the rocks beneath their feet to begin to rumble. In the twinkle of an eye, the army's collective eye will open in time to see itself stop strutting around inside the walls of a marginalized Post Modern Jericho that has already begun to tumble.

Because of that sinking feeling, that army will have no choice but to acknowledge the scientific reality of the fall that it is in the midst of experiencing. On the way down, there will be no way to avoid realizing, in the game of cosmic whist, that the "sound of one hand clapping" is only half of the story. The other half stems from the nature of the zero – which is routinely overlooked. Since it is one zero, it cannot help but sum up to be 1. Philosophically speaking, that sound reasoning turns that one hand clapping into the two (0 and 1) that sound like one clapping because the divine hand is trump tight.

On the way down, the logic in the premise <u>Cogito Ergo Sum</u> (I think, therefore I am) will be upgraded to reflect the objective reality of the alternate basic premise "I think therefore **thought is – whether I am or not"**. Concomitantly, refusing to acknowledge that the Word at center stage in

Genesis is the quintessential example of an objective reality, and the only way to the ultimate reality, becomes a thing of the past. In the process, the term "bottomless pit" will come to be seen as a metaphor for any premise that, in reality, is baseless.

While the gravity of their plight is sinking in, that army of intellects will begin to see gravity (through a glass darkly) as possibly being the unifying field out of which order had to proceed in its translation into light. And light had to precede matter, just as matter had to precede the formation of the orbs, micro and macro, generating the sound of the spheres. The irony is that it would take a falling into outer darkness for an army of inverted intellects to begin to see the light.

As the gravity of the situation continues sinking in, it may be easier for that army to grasp the cosmic significance of the fact that the four words; truth, reality, order, and light, are synonymous terms. Just as any side of a four sided pyramid presupposes the existence of the other three, the use of either of those terms means that the other three apply as well. And since the truth is the light, and the light is the manifestation of that truth, the circular reasoning inherent in the configuration of those four ethereal elements, in effect, comprises the ethereal atom which is analogous to the one that is the building block of matter.

Truth presupposes that the math had already been done prior to arriving at the truth expressed into existence by the order to "Let there be light...". The light intrinsic in the math had to precede the efflux of visible light sent showering in every direction of the cosmic aftermath. Since the creation was accomplished by the expression of the archetypal Word, its byword, the ethereal atom, even though it cannot be seen by the physical eye, is just as much of an absolute as the zero. After all, zero is not nothing. It is a word.

The reason that absolute is above and beyond debate is because there never has been, is not now, and never will be, a debate that can begin without (at least tacitly) bowing the knee to the reality of that ethereal atom. The reason the carnal mind cannot see either the ethereal atom or the fact that it is an absolute is because, by fiat, it has cut itself off from reality by mistaking manifestations of reality for reality itself. Since any objection to the declaration of the existence of the ethereal atom can only be expressed by means of language which features that atom, not only is the tongue of the carnal mind rendered mute, but in the process, new meaning is given to the word mutation.

Accordingly, "In the beginning was the Word..." besides being the opening phrase of the fourth gospel, is the declaration of a universal law. Unlike the law of gravity, which can be superceded by the law of aerodynamics, that universal law is a cosmic axiom from which nothing is exempt. Not a single strand of DNA, a single celestial body, or a single sentence of a body of thought could have begun without the Word. A controlled scientific study will show that there can be no scientific study without the word. That eternally immutable law cannot be broken. Without the Word, even Genesis could not be. The Word is the ubiquitous imperative. Not to know this is blindness.

That being the case, by following the logic innate in the scientific method (which is solely but not exclusively the property of the Logos), inhabitants of the aftermath, which is creation, can only come to one conclusion. The only plausible inference that can be drawn from the answers in Genesis about that state of affairs is that the Bible is the only math book in the world. All others are products of the aftermath.

Since it is impossible to do the math, which, by definition, "hath" already been done, skeptics can do the logical or numerical aftermath. If that seems to be too much like "thinking God's thoughts after Him", the intellectual elite can use the cranial calorie-burning bushes entombed inside their skulls to get a grip on the fact that that Mosaic symbolism was used long before Moses had any way of knowing how apt that burning bush metaphor would come to be in the future. The question as to how Moses could know that his own cranial burning bush was made in the image and likeness of the one that gave him his marching orders is not answered in Genesis directly, but, without too much trouble, an inference can be drawn. The choice of the symbol was made by a burning bush that knew something Moses didn't know.

If elite intellects had raised that question, and pondered the answer arrived at by perusing Genesis, the landscapes of academia might be more presentable. Instead, they are strewn with intellectual nonsense, philosophical foolishness, and myth-infested garbage like the theory of evolution.

That pipedream speculation is far too inane to qualify as a legitimate theory. The reality is that it is a self-immolating absurdity that would have spontaneously aborted itself over a century ago had it not been for the deceit, the frauds, and the pseudoscientific intervention of pseudoscientific parasites on the body of naturalistic knowledge. When it comes to having their primordial pool of brainslime propped up by what they think is law, they are most certainly not pro-choice. When it comes to seeing to it that their mess remains unflushed, they are vehemently proactive. (That speaks volumes about the rules they routinely mistake for law.)

As a matter of fact, that pool of rotten eggheads don't know anymore about what is (and what is not) law than they do about what is (and what is not) choice. Perfection was choice until the fall into imperfection. Choice chose change – hence chance. Then all was chance until the first advent of Jesus the Christ... who is the personification of truth. With the implantation of the truth of the resurrection in the historical time line, chance began the long process of drying up. Eventually, all that remains will be choice once again. The exponential growth of any rootless "figment" tree, secular or religious, is towards drying up. (The word, being an encapsulation of truth, reality, order and light, is the seed of the tree of life.)

Where chance (a prime factor in the theory of evolution) does exist, it presupposes a defection from the state of perfection where all that was could only be choice. In the cosmic sense, defection and devolution are synonymous terms. Ipso facto, the origin of evolution had to lie in the slime of the primordial pool that is a Post Modern myth concocted by eggheads who can't see the difference between evolution and devolution. Taking poetic license with science is usurping a liberty which can only lead to the scientific licentiousness that is bound to boomerang.

That statement is not an assertion... it is an accusation. One way to attempt to refute it would be to intellectually demolish the idea that there can be any such thing as perfection. Such an attempt could only result in an evolutionist having to come face to face with his worst nightmare… an open invitation to find an imperfection in the word "Word". That Word is located at the center of the stage in Genesis – (onto which it had to descend.)

The word cannot be the result of a chemical reaction in the cranial burning bush because there is no reaction that does not presuppose an initiating act. The logical assumption is that the power, the will, and the creative act, must have preceded the chemicals required for there to be any chemical reaction. It follows, then, that the theory of evolution would be a howl if that kind of garbage didn't smell so foul that no self respecting mouth would expose itself to its stench by opening to laugh. It is a well kept secret that that mess spontaneously spawned the Post Modern philosophical bilge espousing the glories of the self-esteem-inducing "will to power". The carnage caused by the ramifications of that bad idea, aside from causing the pages of recent history books to gush blood, also caused torrents of intellectual stupidity to run existentially rampant.

(By the way, thesis and antithesis can never synthesize their way to truth. Truth precludes there being any antithesis of an ideal that is not merely an absence of truth. Since absence is impotence – powerless to synthesize with anything – that advocacy of pluralistic relativism is a thesis that is full of Post Modern, secular humanistic, nonsense.

Critiquing "pure reason" – an oxymoron – is an exercise in Post Modern futility. By its very nature, reason is always once removed from that which it is the reason for. A tome that critiques that which is once removed, as though it were "the thing itself", is really a critique of itself. Reasoning, a process, can be pure, but reason is merely a relatively pure echo that harkens back to that which is sound. So, there are times when a book can be adjudged by its cover to be full of foolish nonsense.

Struggling to exert a "will to power" without realizing that "thy will be done" is the only way to tap into power is an illustration of a woeful lack of an understanding of the issues involved. Had the dynamics of power been understood, an utterance like "God is dead" would never have been allowed to burst forth out into the cultural milieu. The common-sense that seques from essence would immediately have exposed an idea that rejects the existence of a cosmic ideal as being utter nonsense.

Those are but a small sample of the ideas that are considered to be mountain peaks of philosophical endeavor. They were all destroyed by the ideas incidental to the ideal preached in the epistles of Paul. So, the lot of them had already been proved to be no more than foothill footstools before ever they were put into tomes. In this era of devolving Post Modernism, few levelings of philosophical peaks can be made any more plain. Those footstool failures were written off by the Bible before ever they were written out.)

A Juxtapositioning of the "will to power" with the will to "Truth", from which all power must proceed, would have revealed the fact that the taxonomical gap between power and might is every bit as wide as the one between the 1 and the 2. Though that kind of idolatrous foolishness, disguised as philosophy, was able to wreak the bloody (and intellectual) havoc that still resounds, in the process it consigned itself to the garbage heap in the cosmic cul-de-sac where the maggot dieth not.

For a time, after the spigot has been cut off, the hose still holds a little water, but not enough to make the sprinklers spin. For a time, a chicken without a head can flop around the barnyard, but its time is short. For a time, the fangs of the decapitated head of a snake can still inject poison, but the head can't crawl. For a time, mop up skirmishes may still continue, but the cultural war is over.

As words are properly defined, and terminology standardized, pseudoscientific diction is interdicted. Brainwashing is seen to be a function of the Bible. Misinformation dispensed by indoctrinating outlets such as school systems, movies, and media of various "skeezer" stripes, is seen to be the outspouting of brainslime. As smokescreening clouds dissolve, a spade can be called a spade. Pseudoscientific spend-doctors [sic], adepts at switchcraft, can be identified as the academic warlocks that they are – and labeled as such.

Just as vampires cannot stand the light of day, neither can the manufacturers of bogus fossil evidence stand the light of methodically scientific scrutinizing. When those ivory tower charlatans are confined to a spotlight, and not allowed to switch the subject, they are a highlight reel of what it looks like to be "posterized" while caught in the act of being rendered mute.

In the ensuing silence, it may be stated without fear of rebuttal that science which contradicts omniscience is not science. Until they are decoded and embraced as science, faith will be necessary to believe in some of the answers in Genesis. But faith in God is already well on the way to becoming a thing of the past. As it is realized that the vehicle of expression at center stage in Genesis is an empirical objective reality, it is also realized that such an exalted cosmic position presupposes that the Tetragrammaton has to be the ultimate reality. The reason that faith in God is becoming a thing of the past is that there is no need for faith when it is common knowledge that the Godhead is **the quintessential scientific fact.**

Furthermore, the cosmos is so constructed that it is impossible to even attempt to disprove that scientific fact without simultaneously proving the universal validity of that scientific fact. Any attempt to conceptualize the meaning of the "I am" presupposes that it is a replication of the great "I AM" making the attempt. Since there can be no replication without a replicator, that is proof of the Father. The ability to express any idea, pro or con, about that which has been conceptualized is proof of the Son. The truth of the indissolubility of the relationship between the Father and the Son is so indissoluble from Truth that the Father, the Son, and the Spirit of Truth, comprise one Holy Trinity. The answer to the question of why that triune accord is not already accepted as a cosmic axiom may easily be found in Genesis.

Delusions about the existence of God did not begin with a serpent slithering out on the limb of that forbidden tree. The snake had to be a believer in God to rebel against Him.

Delusion came into the picture with belief in the snake. The pair of believers fell from illumination into the shadows resulting from the dis-pairing of their eyes. That peculiar type of blindness increased during the long devolution that, over time, came to be viewed as evolution. Unaware of that ancestral inversion of vision, a portion of their progeny bought into the Post Modern delusion that they tenaciously defend to this day. Highly favored by societies they have indoctrinated into their neo-pagan belief systems, they have roped themselves into having to try to defend a philosophy of science that is as dopey as it is indefensible.

Since they failed to avail themselves of the restoration of vision which occurred at the resurrection of absolute truth, foolish dupes see those who did, and do, bow the knee to the cross as the ones who are deluded. They perceive those who believe the answers in Genesis as the enemy.

Actually, for those who did avail themselves of the cure, things are looking up. Assertions that there is no such thing as an absolute are well on the way to becoming obsolete. As other inane assertions follow suit, it cannot help but become clear that the real adversary of psuedoscientists is the Word at center stage in Genesis. Ask Saul of Tarsus whether or not it is a fearsome thing to fall into the hands of that adversary.

As delusion is compelled to raise its sights, it cannot avoid becoming aware of the signs of the super-intelligence behind the cosmic design. It will become obvious that all that has to happen for the rest of the world to be able to witness the downfall of delusion is for the intelligence (that was not supposed to exist) to remove its foot from the cosmic brakes. Clearly, delusion cannot help but see, at this point, that it is by design that it must make up its mind to either cease and desist, or begin its slide down into the pit where no bottom is to be seen. Obviously, that overview had to have been specifically designed to give the deluded a preview of the fate that awaits those who elect to continue to view the Tetragrammaton as a delusion.

Whether it is admitted or not, anyone with a functioning conscience knows that the only place that science can have a root is in omniscience. And anyone with a cranial burning bush that functions can figure out why omniscience presupposes the omnipresence of omnipotence. By logical extension, the mere presence of the Word at Centerstage in Genesis presupposes the power that, of a truth, is innate in that triune accord. Of a truth, there is no word that does not presuppose a speaker.

The reality of that harmonious accord is so basic that its dynamics are replicated every time a mouth utters a word. The expression of a thought is a deed. Thought, word, and deed (or misdeed), is a Trinitarian affair that no one in the universe can argue about… or without. So, it's a sure bet that anyone made aware of those dynamics and still claiming not to see how foundational The Trinity is has made a tactical decision that it is advantageous to feign ignorance. The idea behind the feint is to delay the fact finding proceedings long enough to amass a heap of impertinent ideas to be thrown on the table for time consuming debate. The hope is for an increase in the density of clouds contributing to the furtherance of religious and scientific confusion.

When the logic intrinsic in the scientific method is brought to bear on the objections to reason at the heart of those clouds, and the confusion blown away, there stands the universal singularity. Enthroned at centerstage in Genesis, it remains the cosmic ideal. Even the foremost among agenda-driven tacticians cannot escape having to bow the knee to the fact that it is as illogical to suppose that any idea can supercede the cosmic ideal as it is to suppose that logic can supercede the Logos.

The fact that all those questionable eggs were put into one highly visible basket full of answers in Genesis was not an accident. Neither was it a tactical error. Even in the culture war, millenniums after the fact, that positioning facilitates the effort to zero in on the basket of answers at issue. At the same time, it diminishes the likelihood of becoming entangled in peripheral issues imported to impede progress toward a final solution. That basket is right up front where every eye can see that if it falls to an academic assault, everything that it stands for must fall with it. But if it continues to stand, nothing that it stands for can fall; and there is nothing that anyone, anything, or any kind of smoke-blowing foolishness in the cosmos can do about it.

It is an understatement to say that the third to last thing that those accustomed to looking through the subjective lens of mental microscopes and telescopes want to see is an issue that can be brought into such sharp focus. Seeing things from a purely objective point of view is devastating to pseudoscientific doctrines. Not only is the concept – "everything is relative" – sealed off from reality, (because that which is real is merely a manifestation of the underlying reality), but that which is absolute is installed, objectively and empirically, on its ethereal throne. When science is properly defined, that throne may be scientifically cited as being the site of the seat of the absolute at centerstage in Genesis.

It is of the universal essence in the cosmic scheme of things that truth, reality, order, and light, would be encapsulated in every word in any language. ("Let there be light..." is one verse. Get it? Uno-verse.) The fact that the meaning behind those four words is represented in every word is as sure as the fact that there are four cardinal directions. In a word, they comprise the supernatural ethereal atom without whose omniscience there would be no such thing as nature, and therefore, no such thing as science. The proof of the veracity of that assertion is that omniscience would be totally unaffected by the absence of either nature or science. Expressed or unexpressed, the omniscience of the Tetragrammaton is an eternal omnipresence.

The generally accepted view of the word (common as grass) may be likened to the generally accepted view of the cell before it was discovered, due to the electron microscope, that the double helix may be the longest word ever spelled. Once that view of chemical spelling (essentially order) is brought into focus, the truth of the reality of that paragon of cosmic order cannot help but to illuminate the reason why truth is a synonymous term for light. And once the brilliance of that light is tempered enough to be focused upon, it becomes easy to see how the word can be seen by man as the Lamb of God at the same time that it is seen as the Lion of Judah by delusion. The fact that the same sentence can mean one thing to the executioner and another to the deluded executee also means that the word is sharper than any two edged sword.

The masterful orchestration of the singular configuration of that state of affairs has to be regarded as either a sure sign of intelligent design, or as a heretofore unheard of instance of "punctuated equilibrium" occurring in the ethereal realm. On its face, such an instance is a contradiction of science, logic and reason, wherever it is alleged to have occurred. It is, in fact, a moronic confabulation whose best chance of every coming anywhere close to being considered a legitimate theoretical issue is for it to self-destruct. So much for that disestablished state of cosmic, as well as comic, delusion.

It is a fundamental error to view God as being merely a superb craftsman when He is really the most consummate artist the universe will ever see. The "very good" creation recorded in Genesis was merely the perfect foundation for trying that which fell into imperfection so that it could be trued. The fact that the potential for imperfection is being exhausted in the process is elevating the original perfection, which was "very good", to the stature of becoming a perfection that is also tried and true. When paradise (re-paired eyes) is restored, the fact that there will be no tree of the knowledge of good and evil in it (because all of its potential has been exhausted) is beautiful. By design, the fact that the whole story of the exhaustion of evil was prerecorded in the Bible will elevate a design that was already a thing of beauty in the beginning to one that will be divinely sublime in the end... "very good", very beautiful, and very true.

The global deluge deposited evidence that it is the nature of delusion to err fundamentally. The delusional mentality is locked into a humanistic worldview that does not allow for the existence of anything that is eternal. Humanistic fundamentalism contributes to the profound blindness which is unable to see that the cosmic scheme of things, since the cosmos is merely a manifestation of an underlying universal reality, precludes there being any reality that is not eternal. Mired in the muck of their fundamental error, deluded dupes are stuck. They would rather continue to believe that clams crawled up to the mountain peaks of the world to become fossilized evidence of a global flood than to recognize the fact that there is a Designer whose majesty is worthy of all the adoration inherent in an awestruck admission to God that "Thou art".

A manifestly truncated little delusional mind trying to tell the Master Designer how to run his art business is like a guppy pup trying to convince an IRS agent that he is entitled to a deduction because he is the head of a human household. The very thought is as ludicrous as any delusional idea designed to impugn the authority and/or authenticity of the cosmic ideal at centerstage in Genesis. The second to last thing that a bunch of lobbyists for a higher wall of separation between church and state wants to hear is that according to Genesis, like it or not, the whole universe is a theocracy. The last thing they want to hear is that there is nothing anybody can do about it.

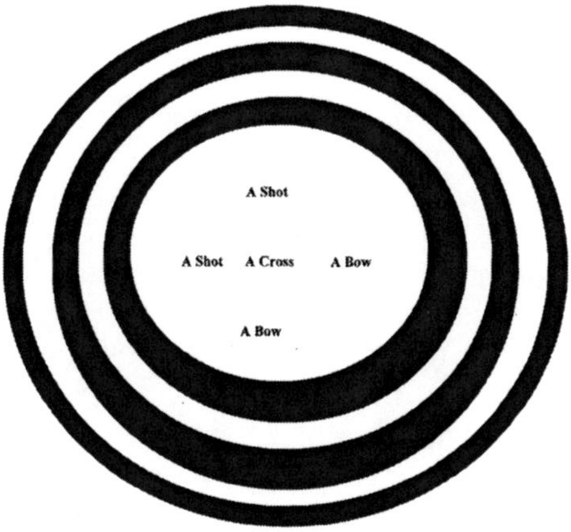
A Shot
A Shot
A Cross
A Bow
A Bow

This section is a target for scoffers looking for points to refute. If they wish, readers who are already believers may skip this section and go on to the next.

The claim this shot across the bow makes is that there is no theology, philosophy, thesis, postulation, or assertion, that attempts to dethrone, demote, or demean Jesus the Christ as deity that is not either ignorant of the issues involved or guilty of propagating a lie – be that lie inadvertent or demonic. Because Jesus is both the Son of man and the linguistic sun of man, and is therefore the Light of the world, there is no way to attempt to deny that Light without becoming living proof that that Light cannot be denied. Because darkness cannot extirpate light, it is rendered mute.

So any mutant that attempts to deny that the Word is an objective reality as well as the ubiquitous imperative is (like the theory of evolution) its own proof that it is a lying foot-stool. The upshot is that any scoffing attempter who fails to refute the points that are made, by that failure, mutates into either a convert or a target. Thus, either way, that upshot is the downfall of that mutant's scoffing.

It used to go without saying that order of any kind presupposed that an order of some kind had already been established. The only alternative to that presupposition is the assumption that order can arise from the random activity of disorder. Aside from the fact that such an assumption turns the universe inside out, it may also fail to take into account the fact that order is hard-wired into the brain. (If it takes it into account, it assumes order evolved.) If order, of a magnitude that it is difficult to imagine, had not been hard-wired into each cell of the brain, there would be no presuppositions or assumptions one way or the other, because there would be no way to order the thinking necessary to arrange the wording of either a postulation or a rebuttal. There was a time when laying a foundational preamble before attempting a foray into rationality would have been considered superfluous. Since it used to be obvious that the universe is not turned inside out, order was intuitively accepted as a given. My, how times have changed.

In this Post Modern age, a new strain of old hat, wipe-the-slate-clean, skepticism has emerged to take the bit in its mouth. This mutant has determined that, once a certain intellectual height has been attained, there are no givens. In certain of their lofty schools of thought, commonsense issues, which used to be viewed as no-brainers, can be, and often are, regarded as unwarranted assumptions. Breathing, for instance, (once a sure sign of existence) is a no-brainer no more.

Quite likely, it was foreseen by well-stipened, pragmatic, "survival of the fittest" theorists that the dogmatic constraints inherent in a given would become a bigger problem than it already was if something were not done. Already, the synthesized schools of thought (ancient and modern – Eastern and Western) that they were herding into place, as the foundational schematics for their proposed Humanistic Utopia, were being threatened by mental midgets seeking to apply the reasoning of the given-based intellectual commoner to an uncommonly pragmatic undertaking. It is well known that too many cooks spoil the broth. What is not so well known is that the democratic process, simply because it is democratic, has too many cooks. Uncurbed, the given was bound to drive carefully laid plans to a terminal case of apoplexy. The given had to be taken.

So, commonsense presuppositions (breathing equals existing) that it once would have been ludicrous to question were shrouded in clouds of philosophic conceptualizations that had been teased into the elegantly designed facades that erode trust in anything other than the polemic cul de sacs strategically constructed along lines laid out by the white papers routinely spawned by agenda-driven, think tank, intellection. Modern technology has allowed the dictates of those highly evolved social engineers to span the globe far more swiftly than in times past when even a village idiot accepted the postulation that the difference between an anal sphincter and a hole in the ground was, without question, a given. And, without question, the directive has gone out to transform the global village into a collective of idiots who are quite willing to go along with the hypothesis that, since nothing is absolute, nothing can be a given.

So it came to be on that high plane where the "high priests of intellect", in collaboration with the superstar "gurus of the moment", concoct the trend-setting tenets that are sent down to the social engineers who stir those learned opinions into the crosscurrents of nebulous "ologies" and "isms" aimed at fostering an increase in the New Age rash of mental hung juries, that recipes for netherworldly pots of half digested gruel began to be drafted. By means of the Sunday morning filibuster, the computer-brewed drafts are spewed out on the occupants of pews and passed on, during the rest of the week, to captive audiences kept under academic lockdown in desk chairs. The gist of the draftings is then spin doctored so it will easily trickle all the way down into the eye-bopping, ear-boxing, cartoons that screw day-crawling rugrats down into TV screenside seats. With dazzling arrays of digitalized color and stereophonic sound, that ghoulish mishmash of mix and match mess is funneled into the eyes and ears of mesmerized innocents... to ferment... subliminally.

It is through such soil, fertilized by degrees, that two streams of thought flow on their way to merge into the New Age mainstream which feeds the rising tide of an idea whose time, apparently, has arrived. From headwaters in the East streams the postulation that all is an illusion. From headwaters in the West, snaking its way around the dam emblazoned with cogito ergo sum, that stream pools, primordially, around the infinitesimally small feat of the Big Bang.

When extended to their logical conclusions, the Western ideology which, when it does not succumb to the fatalistic malaise resulting from the Eastern belief that all is an illusion, is primed to fall prey to the "might makes right", pragmatic, outlook whose mascot motto is "survival of the fittest". (That outlook, by the way, is diametrically opposed to the beatitude which dogmatically states that "The meek shall inherit the earth".) Both philosophical outlooks imply that resistance is futile, but one does so from a position of self-induced imagined weakness, while the other does so from a position that exaggerates its own imagined strength. As representations of reality, both views are one, in that, being imaginary, neither is fit to survive.

You'd never know it, though, by listening to the roundtable of TV talkshow scoffers as they roundly pillory the idea of an "objective reality" and the "religious nonsense" that such an antiquated idea continues to foster. (An objective reality would have to be a given, and that comes dangerously close to presupposing a giver.) According to that august group, if the idea of an objective reality can be subjected to questioning, it follows that it has to be at least as subjective as it is objective, which makes it as much an oxymoronic contradiction in terms as a blue orange or a grape nut. But then, according to them, that is precisely the type of flaky, fluky, fruit one would expect to find on the table of intellectually challenged hoi polloi who have yet to evolve far enough to be able to see that a given, where all is illusion, has to also be an illusion.

With reasoning like that, is it any wonder that an individual who has been systematically mainstreamed to believe that truth, besides being subjective, is also a commodity that can be individually possessed? Your "own truth" can be anything anybody says it is. That species of "muddying the waters" cannot help but shade shady areas even more; and that shading blurs the boundaries between that which is true and that which is not so true even more. Confusion being added to confusion is a prelude to getting rid of boundaries entirely.

There can be little doubt that erasing boundaries, like getting rid of givens, helps to pave the way for the acceptance of evolution, not as a theory, but as a proven fact. There can be no doubt that a "survival of the fittest" attitude encourages a lack of respect for the not so strong dogs at the same time that it encourages a healthy respect for the dogs that are on top. And there is no doubt that the top dogs, with all the big money to be made in building dog pounds, have a vested interest in seeing manageable portions of the population act like dogs.

Nor is there the least bit of doubt, with the assistance of the superior "You've come a long way, baby". court, that the removal of boundaries has gone a long way toward bringing the "question" of the normal and natural use of certain body orifices into the arena of public debate (serious debate) on prime time TV. It is not surprising that a climate which fosters the abolition of the given will dovetail nicely with fostering the abolition of the line between genders. Since there is no question why a median strip divides a highway, the question should be: What is there to question? A bent gender is bent.

There was a time in the early years of the "powers of the air" generation when a semi- nude body undulating across a TV screen would have caused federal licensing bodies to fall off their thrones in their efforts to reach one of the phones they use to make sure that a head rolls. Those licensing bodies, having rapidly evolved to the point where they take great pains to protect the right to hold onto your "own truth", now fall off their thrones when a christmas decoration is displayed on a village green. Today, envelope-pushing commercial messages semi-nudely and semi-subtly striving for the breakthrough that will allow open pandering to the pedophilic market are winked at; but the mere mention of one of the Ten Commandments within a hundred yards of a classroom is enough to turn an idle throne room phone into a federal case hotline.

By juxtaposing that which is slyly winked at with that which is scowlingly pounced upon, and by making use of a little commonsense while pondering that juxtaposition, anyone who can connect dots can see that some licensing bodies are in the business of licensing licentiousness. Then, by drawing the inferences, it is possible to see "tap dancing" puppets put on their shows for free. As a matter of fact, an attentive ear can tell by the tapping of the dance steps that somewhere up the chain of command there is a white paper explaining why the deregulation of regulating bodies is a necessary step toward creating the ashes which are a must if the New Age phoenix is to arise.

So, what at first glance might appear, to the utterly naïve, to be a federal case of benign neglect which just happened to leave a door ajar for creeping porn to seep in, upon second glance, to the no longer naïve, appears to be neither negligence nor benign. Rather, the winking of the federal eye is a key strategic cog in the sinister machinations advancing the humanistic order gone out to facilitate and expedite the idolization of the clone and the cyborg as the crowning glory of evolution.

Since neither the clone nor the cyborg is a given, but a construction, it has to be inferred that anything which even remotely can be construed as a given is a philosophical, logical, and logistical roadblock that can only serve to hinder any attempt at Post Modernization. Far from blurring boundary lines, the given makes what is on either side of the line stand out in stark contradistinction. It makes it easy to see that: "YES, Virginia, there is a line…"; and that it could not have been drawn more clearly. Any given, to the extent that it represents reality, presupposes a giver. And a giver presupposes that evolution, as foisted, is a fraud. That which gives, and that which evolves, cannot coexist as coequals. Any gender that is not bent knows that a washer isn't a nut. That's just commonsense.

XXXXXX

According to the TV guide, the title of the debate was: The Scientific Evolution of Reason Over the Illusion of Existance. The Commoner, an advocate of commonsense, planned to find a way to get into the studio; not so much to advocate as to find out what such an imposing billing actually meant. Recently, after coming across the term "circular reasoning", he had been doing quite a bit of thinking about reason. The more he looked at it, the more it was beginning to seem that reason was not what it was cracked-up to be. The way it seemed like it ought to be, is that reasoning is the process of arriving at an explanation. Once an explanation has been arrived at... that would be the reason. Neither the abstract process of arriving at an explanation, nor the explanation itself, is a natural entity. (Every explanation is abstracted from whatever it explains.) So, if science is only supposed to concern itself with natural, observable, phenomena, why would a panel of scientific thinkers be debating what is clearly a supernatural issue?

Having already donned one of those jackets with patches sewn on the elbows, The Commoner, looking preoccupied, rummaged through drawers, searching for a pipe. He was trying to marshall the irrefutable evidence needed to support his thesis that a simple "I am" should be sufficient proof that he existed. Judging by the subject matter of the debate, the fact that he was so certain of his existance should, in itself, be enough to get him inside – maybe not to advocate for commonsense or anything like that, but just to ask a question or two about reason as it relates to evolution and illusion.

As expected, the security guard posted to check credentials was caught off-guard by the scholarly sounding term "Principle of Superfluity". Instead of having a credential waved at him as though he was the latest generation of an a t m, he was being let in on what, presumably, was a recent lecture. As the guard mentally reset himself, The Commoner winked and began to point out to him that, in order for anyone to be granted the right to enter, that one would have to exist merely to be informed that no one could enter without being granted the right to enter. For that reason alone, having to go all the way back home to pick up a credential was not only degrading to his existance, but a perfect example of the Principle of Superfluity, also.

Readily admitting the reasonableness of that thesis, the guard pointed out that he had been hired to do a job, and he fully intended to do it. But he considered it unreasonable (pocketing the bill) to be held responsible for checking credentials at the front door, and, at the same time, be held responsible for an intrusion by any undocumented person it might occur to to go around to the rear door that had been left ajar, presumably, for purposes of ventilation. People as smart as that crew inside should know that one man cannot be in two places at the same time. But, he said with a wink, to say anymore than that would probably be just another example of the principle of superfluity.

Though the show was not yet on the air, the pre-debate banter was already in progress. While the members of the panel all appeared to be cut from the same cloth, not everyone was personally acquainted with everyone else, so it was not obvious to anyone that The Commoner, though a bit young, was not just as distinguished a member of the august panel as everyone else. The Commoner signaled the doctor of philosophy to go on making his point as he sat down to listen.

It did not take long for the newcomer to become aware that those around the table were generally agreed that it was imperative that the slate be wiped clean of all the old philosophical contructs. As he understood it, they were all agreed that the intelligence of the old world giants was of a lesser quality than their own; — if for no other reason than the lack of the high-tech quantity that is the hallmark of the New Age. There could be no standing on the shoulders of giants who, due to no fault of their own, had been turned into dwarfs simply by the passing of time. As The Commoner understood it, their position was: until it was proved by the application of reason that standing on shoulders was not as superfluous as an appendix, they were resolved to stand on no shoulders at all. Newly evolving scientific premises had to be erected on the rock hard foundation of pure reason.

Though an eyewitness to the scene, it was still hard for The Commoner to believe it was possible that a time could come when it would be necessary to look back in time in order to find that there had once been a time when "standing on the shoulder of giants" was taken so much for granted that the attitude of appreciation which goes along with that realization was a given. Hard to believe or not, judging by the low-level imperiousness of the august panel, it was more than apparent that just such time had arrived. Not wanting to appear as though he had come into the room spoiling for a fight, and resisting the urge to point out that it seemed to him that Achilles would have had to be an arachnid to supply enough heels for the holes in their wipe-the-slate-clean propositions, The Commoner just listened.

Since he was really just thinking out loud, it is possible he would not have been heard saying that reason is not an entity if those words hadn't fallen neatly into the gap of silence between the alert that it was air time and the panel composing itself to go on camera. Probably, it was because their attention was on assuming a more upright posture that their jaws did not drop. Or, it might have been that they could not bring themselves to believe what they thought they had heard. Immediately after his opening few words, the moderator, also cut from the same cloth, graciously smoothed the way for a quick recantation by asking Mr. ____ (Of course, The Commoner's name was not in his notes. He supplied it.) —– Mr. Commoner if he wished to elaborate.

Mindful that they were on the air, and wishing to clarify his meaning in as succinct a manner as possible so that he could resume listening, The Commoner enlarged on the statement by saying that the only kind of entity reason could possibly be is one that is abstract. Reason is dependent upon the entity rather than being independent of the entity; so, while it is a factor, it is not, and cannot be, the fact itself. Since it is not a fact, but a factor, it cannot be a foundation. If reason were to be a foundation, then reason, as a foundation, would have to be the reason for reason. As an illustration, he used the formula $E = MC^2$; saying that it is not the formula but the bomb that is the entity — until it is exploded — then it would cease to be an entity also. After the mushroom cloud... blue-sky. Then he hurried to say that what he was really more interested in was hearing what the distinguished panel had to say; — especially about the "illusion" of existance.

Perhaps, to give his colleagues time to assimilate the import of what had been said and prepare their rebuttals, the moderator refused to be hurried. He thought he had heard what was said, but he wasn't sure that he had understood it. He asked The Commoner if he could be a little more specific.

The Commoner chose a ladder to further illustrate the point he was attempting to make. The way he saw it, each rung represents a reason. An accumulation of valid reasons allows leaves to be cleaned out of the gutter. Climbing is the reason for ladders. The rungs, step by step, are the reason that ladders can be climbed. Climbing, step by step, is the reasoning process used to arrive at the reason for the climb… cleaning out the gutters. But if the gutters had been cleaned the previous day, both the reasoning and the reason become superfluous. They vanish. Like the bomb, they become blue-sky.

Hoping to combat what he saw in the panel of faces as further confusion, The Commoner went on to explain that attempting to base a system of thought on reason alone would be like laying a ladder on the ground and running to and fro on its rungs. That might be an exhibition of reasoning ability, but it would also be like a musician practicing scales.

Practicing scales is not music; and running back and forth on a horizontal ladder won't get the gutters clean. The point is, that without a point, not only is reason pointless, but, for all practical purposes, it is unreasonable, and, therefore, non-existant. Blue-sky.

Aware that if he had not made the point as clear as it needed to be, it would confuse the issue, The Commoner hurried to say that he had not meant to infer that reason and reasoning did not exist; only that they do not exist independent of an objective. To be sure, at times, reason may resolve issues, but reasoning itself tells anyone willing to listen that it can never correct a problem, because it can never directly address it. It can't get to the root. The rays of the sun are not the reason for the sun. The sun is the reason for the rays. Though the rays lead to the sun, they can never be the sun. By the same token, just as rays would be non-existant without the sun, so is a specific reason non-existant without that which it is the reason for. It only stands to reason that reason cannot be the reason for reason. That would be circular reasoning.

It occurred to the Commoner that he might be monopolizing air time; but he also knew that he might not have taken up as much time as he thought. Since the moderator didn't stop him, he went on to explain that reason is not a source; but a resource. It is a re-sounding of that from which it emanates, be that source sound or unsound: therefore, in and of itself, reason can neither be accurate nor inaccurate, because it merely echoes what is. A reason for a success is fully as much a reason as a reason for failure. Neither success nor failure has any bearing. Reason cannot be upgraded, downgraded, or degraded; because it does not carry the necessary weight to be given a grade of its own. It never tells "what"; – only "why."

Trying to sound scientific rather than sarcastic, he went on: A zero is a circular hole. A reason without an antecedent is a zero. To sweep the slate clean in order to try to erect a philosophy based on pure reason, since pure reason is a hole, is to try to build a body of thought on circular reasoning; — which is a pure hole. At best, it would be a baseless philosophy… a superfluity which, being a nothing, cannot be present to stand on the shoulders of the giants standing on the slate rather than over the hole; — from the bottom of which, reputedly, there evolved an extremely big, begging-the-question, bang. What is begged of the question is the answer to how a Big Bang could possibly come bustin' out of nothing with nothing to initiate the ignition of the combustion but the decree that there was a Big Bang. When recognized as the superfluity that it is, that question is begged in vain.

Thus, the best case scenario for the evolution of the superfluity would have been its failure to evolve. Were it to somehow continue to evolve, the more it evolved, the worse off it would be. The circular reasoning at its core could not help but evolve into a whirling black hole. Any superfluity with baselessness for a foundation, ultimately, must be left in suspension over just such a hole.

Trying to put an end to what was becoming a soliloquy, The commoner had a question ready for the panel at the end of the commercial break. What he wanted to know was – If all is an illusion, in scientific terms, what were the dynamics of the process of natural selection that accounted for the evolution of the eye. He took it for granted that the panel did not question the existance of the eye; — since sight is necessary to see that an illusion is an illusion. Apparently, they could see where that question was leading, and needed a bit of time to devise a roadblock. But that left the "dead air" The Commoner felt obligated to fill in order to take the onus off the moderator who, it must remembered, was cut from the same cloth as the panel.

He swiftly came up with an instance that, hopefully, would clarify the position they would need to block. He purposely sought to be even more low-key when he began to explain that just as there can be no way of standing under a shade tree without standing in the shade, no stance can be taken for (or against) anything unless that thing, like that tree, is understood to exist. To take a stand for (or against) the existance of illusion, is to presuppose that the sight exists to make that determination. If sight exists, its very existance proves that existance is not an illusion. So, its just commonsense to deduce that there would have been no slate to be swept clean in the second place, if, in the first place, all had been an illusion; — not to mention the fact that, in the third place, without sight, there would have been no way of seeing if the slate was an illusion or not. So, to repeat the question, what he wanted to know was how natural selection could select from what was not even there to be selected from to evolve an eye.

He did have the presence of mind to refrain from adding; — it is a peculiar brand of shortsightedness that seeks to sweep the slate clean in order to base a theory on a hole. It just stands to reason that no reason can ever be pure reason, because no reason can ever be sound unless it re-sounds. If it re-sounds, it is really an echo. Without a sound, an echo is pure, cloudless, blue-sky, nothing.

Just at the time of the next break, The Commoner (mistakenly) felt he was beginning to get through to the august group. And, after the break, he was somewhat encouraged when one member of the panel said it was all merely a matter of semantics. The reason he was encouraged was because he considered it an absolute necessity to get through the semantics in order for him to get at the point that he was trying to make. However, what most called semantics, he called seam-antics and/or seem-antics. He explained: — finding a seam between a word and its true etymological meaning; prying that seam apart and filling it with the meaning the "pryer" wanted it to have; and making a word seem to mean whatever that "pryer" wanted it to mean, was very close to getting to the crux of the problem. But, he was discouraged when that member of the panel cut him off to say that The Commoner had his "own truth", and they had theirs. It was not clear if "they" meant the "pryer", the panel, or both.

Perhaps, while he still had some presence of mind, that would have been the ideal moment to recognize the fact that he was getting nowhere, and retreat into total silence. After everything he said had been glossed over, toward the end of the show he could have asked an innocuous question or two, and then joined in ending the show with an engaging smile at the lens of the camera. But, before he could stop himself, he had already told the panel that having their "own truth" was the only way they could get away with that "stuff". By "stuff" (he clarified before being asked to do so) he meant using the strata of rock to determine the age of the fossils found in that layer — until it becomes expedient to do the scientifically relativistic, revisionist, switcheroo; and making a u-turn to use the age of the fossils in the rocks to determine the age of the strata. He managed to soften his tone somewhat as he told them that, besides being circular reasoning, which is unreasonable and unconscionable, the whole construct, (based on a pseudo-scientific "geological column" that does not exist anywhere on earth), was also a bunch of hooey.

With the case having already been made, perhaps it would have been wise not to put icing on the cake by producing a shortlist of, evolution-supporting, proven frauds gleaned from scientific journals, and passing around photocopied handouts of the documentation. They were what he liked to call examples of the "front page – back page syndrome". It was front page news when the archeological discovery was made, and back page news when the discovery was discredited. His own favorite on the list was Nebraska Man whose ancestral roots had been traced all the way back to a hog's jaw tooth. So, his attempts to address the issue was not purely a matter of semantics anymore than anything in existance can be said to be a matter of pure reason. Parenthetically, he said that pure reasoning will prove there is no such thing as pure reason... one hundred percent of the time. And, he went on to point out, speaking of reason and semantics, he felt he would be derelict if he did not go out of his way to stress the fact that "pure reason", being a contradiction in terms, is unreasonable. Therefore, it cannot be merely a matter of semantics to point out that unreasonableness, in this case, is merely a euphemism for blue-sky dumb. In a nutshell, the pathological philosophy behind that display of unbridled, (but surreptitiously serpentine) exhibition of willfulness is pragmatism. The nature of its pathology is that it thinks it can bend logic without it becoming ill.

Strictly speaking, pragmatism is not one philosophy, but compendiums of the skeletal remains of a wide range of philosophies that have been twisted to fit the agenda of those who consider themselves at or near the apex of the fortunate few that evolution has deemed most fit to survive. Cutting through the semantics, pragmatism is a sort of think tank version of getting down to the level "where the rubber meets the road". It could be called a species of academic street smarts that has been decked out to look like commonsense; — but it is really a perversion. One of its salient features is its willingness to trade a principle for a brownie point; another is its willingness to sacrifice that which is honorable on the altar of expediency in exchange for a desired result. Naturally, its "end justifies the means" methodology makes pragmatism the first cousin of what has been mistakenly dubbed communism. (Real communism is what transpired between Adam and the Creator before the fall; and what transpires between the Creator and the priesthood of believers since the resurrection.)

The aim of the circular reasoning semantically hidden at what would be the heart of pragmatism, if it had one, is supposed to be the upliftment of humanity. Ironically, that evolution would entail being lifted to an acceptable degree of heartlessness. That is why pragmatic victories have a hollow ring. Drippings from the think tank top seep down to the poolhall bottom where it is translated into the vernacular and disseminated as the street smart wisdom that advises: "If you can't make it, shake it." When logically extended, pragmatism's apparent victories are simply "last mile" steps to its eventual demise. The illness inherent in flawed logic certifies that it must come to a dead end before it can reach its intended destination. Believing in its own seam-antics, "in your face" pragmatism, with its "survival of the fittest" attitude, marched out of its subterranean closet...going forth to establish its unreasonably brave new world order. Pragmatic confidence exudes from the swagger of an "idea whose time has come" as it marches off to conquer the sun with the business end of a garden hose held at "present arms".

The Commoner was discovering that it was extremely difficult to find a chink in the armor made with layers of scales fashioned out of refined unreasonableness. Cutting through obfuscating semantics served only to highlight the diametrical opposition between the panel (the red corner), and The Commoner (the blue corner). The panel professed to believe in tolerance for all beliefs — up to and including belief in the lie. On the other hand, The Commoner believed in tolerance of everything except the lie. In the geo-political mind game, which thrives on the art of compromise, and whose influence trickles all the way down into what has become known as street smarts, tolerance for belief in the lie is an absolute necessity. That tolerance has a distinct advantage over the inability to tolerate such a belief because it frees the red corner to bob and weave its way in and out of loopholes, while the blue corner has to stand up for what it believes in. Naturally, that means the blue corner had better be adept at rolling with the punches. Having its "own truth", and priding itself in its ability to tolerate your "own truth", the red corner demonstrates its belief that truth is relative. It is the belief in the relativity of truth that provides the pragmatist with the crawl space needed to squeeze out the wiggle room to do whatever is necessary, and possible, to make sure that it is the "fittest" who survive. The pot of gold at the end of that particular rainbow is the glory that comes with being acclaimed the most highly evolved of the most highly evolved species. The chest-pounding bravado that Tarzan engages in as he lords it over the jungle is engaged in, at a more highly evolved level, by the brave new landlords of the whole earth. Of such are the heights to which tolerance promises to elevate the most fit species the world has ever known; and the pragmatic panel, in the red corner, is, of course, representive of the high evolution of that species.

There is, however, one belief that pragmatists do not believe in tolerating. If your "own truth" happens to be belief in the objective reality of an absolute truth… that belief is verboten: Pragmatists can't abide it… can't stand it… don't like it… won't have it, and whenever and wherever anything like an anachronistic anachronism like dogmatic dogma is found, it must be hunted down, run down, and stomped out. So, it would seem that one of the things that the pragmatists is locked into being dogmatic about is his intolerance of any belief in any dogma. The other thing he is locked into is his insistance that he is tolerant of all beliefs. The result is that preaching tolerance on one hand, and practicing intolerance on the other, is not viewed as hypocritical duplicity, but as the survival of the most fit by any means necessary. So, when the pragmatist is put in the position of having to lie through his clenched teeth, he is also put in the position of clenching his teeth to doggedly hang onto his belief that he is tolerant.

Pragmatists know only too well that there are a dwindling number of those still able to see through their lies because part of their job is to see to it that those numbers continue to dwindle. But, until the numbers can be whittled down into insignificance, they will have to resort to the cover-up. When the cover-up is not extensive enough to hide the way things are going, stern directives are issued, and compliance with them must be enforced. Were it not for those devices and coercive measures, pragmatists would have to come clean. Since coming clean is not a viable option; for the pragmatist, the alternatives are damage control or extinction. If they have anything to say about it, the "fittest" have not survived this long to become extinct.

The cover-up is accomplished by coordinating gala displays of news and other forms of amusing entertainment... in collaboration with federally mandated "education", which, by the way, is also quite amusing. These forms of semantically enhanced mental chloroform are weapons of mass destruction produced by big profitable businesses that help to supply the funds needed to add additional layers to the cover-up. And, of course, deploying the enforcement arm of the pragmatic lie means that concept of your "own truth" has to be abridged, abrogated, or violated, whenever a "fittest" panel decrees that such measures are expedient. Curtailment, abrogation, and violence, then, have to be recognized as justifiable means for bringing about the desired end... a brave new world order whose hallmark will be its devotion to tolerance.

Naturally, coming clean, not being a viable option, is out of the question. Coming clean would mean admitting that there is an absolute truth that is not your own and must be adhered to because it cannot be manipulated. To admit to the existance of such a truth would be like thumping the first domino in an elaborately serpentine pattern designed to the specifications of a new age of unreasonable constructs. Put another way, coming clean would undo the dirt. To the pragmatists, committed to allowing the end to justify the means, that would be a dirty shame.

The Commoner knew that there was an aphorism which, in effect, states that those who go around putting out eyes are themselves blinded in the process. Were it to come about, the coming clean that would be a dirty shame to the pragmatists… to the Commoner, had already come about because the panel was already a dirty shame; and it was a dirty shame that they could not see how unreasonably shameful they were. Fit, well fed, directly and/or indirectly federally funded, they were amply empowered to lay their semantical traps… unaware that they were being trapped by their own semantical manipulations.

Obviously, they had gerrymandered the meaning of the word "tolerance" so that when the meaning of the word "acquiescence" was tailored to fit within the same parameters, and then cloaked to hide the tailoring, either meaning could be used by the "fittest", depending upon which meaning was needed at the time to insure the continued evolution of their survival. Semantically speaking, when your "own truth" clashed with their "own truth", in their own minds, your "own truth" really meant your own acquiescence to the will of the "fittest"... a state of affairs they were quite willing to tolerate. Simply put, though your "own truth" would be valid, their "own truth" would be more valid.

In the process of gerrymandering, the pragmatists have gerrymanded themselves into a position where they must acquiesce to continual lying simply to survive in the fashion they have grown accustomed to. Lying is the only way they can stay fit enough to keep on with their lying. In the parlance of the street: "They gotta be lying." Since lying is a necessary condition of their continued existance, like Pinocchio's nose, their forked tongues must continue to grow longer and longer. However, nature will only permit a tongue to grow so long before it declares that mutation unfit for further evolution: so the semantical magician, bent on creating a world of New Age puppets, is just much of a problem to himself as he is to anyone else.

By no means, on that account, was The Commoner looking for a hand to slap with a high five. Though well aware that he was standing on the shoulders of giants who totally agreed with his contention that he had no "truth" that he could call his own, he was also aware that neither was he on his own turf. He was on the playing field of a panel that did not even have to open its mouth to lie about how tolerant it was because the story was told by its body language. As though it were one portly, pipe-sucking, paunch, simmering with the hostility of pent up, destructive, refutation, the panel anxiously awaited the end of the commercial so that, as one high powered intellect, it could proceed to jab him silly before knocking him out.

True, he had a knockout punch of his own. One absolute truth, such as the fact that there never has been, is not now, and never will be a time when it is not "now", is enough to put an end, not only to all of that my "own truth" – your "own truth" nonsense, but to the whole Humanistic, Post Modern, New Age, stagnant, primordial, pool that thinks it is a movement, when, in reality, it is only a periodic eruption on the pimply face of time. The problem for The Commoner was that it is difficult to deliver a knockout blow to that which, not only is without a foundation, but, in its relativistic drunkenness with the power afforded it by its abolition of the belief in absolute truth, refuses to admit that any foundation it must respect exists. Simply put, the pragmatists have declared that any foundation that does not concur with the finding that they are the most fit to survive is not a foundation. It is an obstacle. To the pragmatist, any opposing view is just a matter of semantics.

The Commoner could see that the strong suit of the pragmatists (their abuse of semantics) was also their weak spot. The same plasticity which allows semantics to be twisted into agenda-driven loopholes is also elasticity waiting to untwist. When stretched to its limit, that elasticity begins the process of overruling the rule imposed by pragmatic semantic liars. The truth is: — just as there would be no such thing as a negative were it not for the positive, there could be no such thing as a lie if there were no truth to bend and twist out of shape.

Like a beaver's dam, now and again, lies have to be shored up. Lies shoring up lies results in a pack of lies. Since it is truth that is the raw material that is bent and twisted into those lies, like a seal visiting a blowhole in the ice for air, now and again, the pragmatic liar (the exact opposite of nobility posing as nobility) has to revisit the truth: — otherwise his pack of lies, like every other construct in the universe, will begin to succumb to the law of entropy. In their disintegration, true constructs disclose that which is true. Lying constructs disclose where and how the truth was bent and twisted out of shape in order to give form to the lie.

"Now" is neither a formation or a construct. It is an absolute, eternal, objective reality that preceded all time, still precedes time, and always will precede time. Commonsense tells anyone willing to listen that that is the way it has to be because time never stops passing, while "now" never starts. Time is a wasting asset, while "now" is as much now as it ever was, or is ever going to be. Time is a construct of man. Nothing else in nature, in their cyclical tours or natural rhythms, pays any attention to it at all. Nature tours in its innate tours… time merely measures the tours that are innate.

"Now" is beyond measure, or measuring. Yet, it is always being pre-sent into the present. Check the semantics.

The fact that the present, and "now", are inextricably linked, besides being commonsense, is an absolute truth that is not scientifically or logically challengable. Though that fact does not have an "attitude", it is "in your face", figuratively and literally, all the time; and would have been "in your face", had "you" had a face, before time – that is to say, eternally. Moreover, it does not matter which direction any face (including theoretical alien faces) faces, "now", is now. When hell freezes over, "now" will be now – (except for the pragmatic semanticist). "Now" will remain "now", but that highly evolved species will have no way of knowing it because when that species faces that fact, and refuses to face up to it, by its own refusal, that species is turned into a "not". Check the logic in the semantics.

As hell freezes over, and the blowholes of that species of seal gradually turns into "not" holes, the craft of finding which hole is still open, and which is not, becomes a matter of survival. Those semantical seals <u>must</u> have more truth to shore up their lies, but the truth is, that in that day of closing loopholes, the blowholes will be turning into "not" holes faster than the lies can be re-packed to replenish the effectiveness of their seam-antics. That icy ceiling, besides redirecting their agendas, will play hell with their attitudes. As the logic of pragmatism is extended, it cannot do anything other than hasten its own doom.

Science, by definition, entails submission to truth. It does not have the slightest problem with admitting that "now" is an absolute truth. Science includes that truth in its body of knowledge. Science readily admits, though "now" is not a physical thing, that it is a metaphysical reality. It is a metaphysical reality that may be repeatedly experimented with because there is never a time when it is not right there in your face to prove that it's not "your truth" — or anyone elses. In other words, it is a truth that is beyond anyone's control. That is an objective reality.

That which calls itself science, but cannot abide the truth of an objective reality, because it refuses to submit to truth, must, by definition, be categorized as a non-science. That which is not science, in the day of closing blowholes, will be revealed for what it truly is... witchcraft. Though that case of Post Modern witchcraft purports to have a brave new agenda, and a brave new "in your face" attitude, it is the same old semantically shrouded, "to taste or not to taste?", forked tongue, foolishness that is being surfaced to face the limits of semantical elasticity. Divide, marginalize, and conquer, is the strategy, which, upon arriving at the limits of semantical elasticity, may either concur with the objective reality of the "now" before the last blowhole is sealed, or, conquered by that icy ceiling, be marginalized and boomeranged to the bottom of waters turning into fire.

Nothing is new about the strategy of marginalizing commoners by backing them into a corner and jabbing them into a sense of intellectual inferiority. The Commoner was backed into just such a corner. He had to admit to the panel that, from kindergarten on, he had never graduated in the top ten percent of any class. And, no, he could not tell them where he had done his postgraduate work. Remembering the advice he had heard TV lawyers give their clients, he did not volunteer the additional information that he hadn't done any post graduate work because he had yet to finish his undergraduate work.

While he was still bristling at the term "intellectual peon" hissed from somewhere to this left, and wondering if he should try to re-introduce some logic into the debate by pointing out the ad hominum tenor of the attack, he was hit with the term "interloper" from somewhere to his right. That member went on to state that it was his opinion that The Commoner was an interloper who, judging by his unimpressive lack of the mastery of the art of circumlocution, was in way over his head, because it certainly seemed as though Mr. Commoner had ventured into an unfortunate foray into an apologetic for the common cause.

Under normal circumstances The Commoner would have called the speaker's attention to the fact that the name of the logical error in his reasoning was a non sequiter, but someone else interjected to ask him (The Commoner) if he didn't know that he (The Commoner) was god, and that the world was only his (The Commoner's) dream. By implication, that speaker, who had his "own truth", was his own god also. That meant, by implication, that The Commoner was only a dream as far as god was concerned: Or better yet, merely an illusion. So the beleaguered Commoner found himself impaled on the horns of a three pronged dilemma.

He knew he was not an illusion because every jab was painful in at least two ways. Besides the pain of the jab itself, there was also the vicarious pain that he felt for the logic that was being twisted into unreasonable illness. And he also knew that if he cried "I am" loud enough to distress the eardrum of the cosmos, all that the high priest in charge of "an idea whose time has come" had to do was tell him to prove it. Then, of course, the proof, no matter how conclusive, would be called hearsay evidence from an illusion, and therefore, would be ruled inadmissible. His defense would amount to no more than any ticket-ee's protestations of innocence in any kangaroo traffic court.

The third prong of the dilemma actually occurred first. How was it possible to counter a <u>non</u> <u>sequiter</u> as a flaw in logic when that logician's basic premise rests on the unreasonable foundation that he has his own truth – a movable feast on a movable foundation that is the logical equivalent of a moving hoop on a moving backboard. The temptation was to get sucked into trying to beat them at their own "survival of the fittest" game; but that, he knew, in the long run, would make him just another pragmatist. However, between the short run and the long run, there can be many punches thrown, which, if not slipped, can cause a lot of blood to be spilled.

He bobbed when he should have weaved, and the jaw-socking, brain rattling, blow smashed through his guard to drive home the point that if any Commoner had the temerity to accuse elite members of an august panel of circular reasoning, then he was automatically guilty of circular reasoning; — otherwise, he never would have made such an accusation, and, therefore, was in need of being knocked out cold. Next came the vicious blow that landed just below the belt line and put him on the seat of his pants. Out of nowhere, someone whom he did not see had asked to see his credentials. Slowly, he toppled over on his side, but he managed to get to his feet at the count of nine. He was saved from the "onward to the slaughter" charge by the commercial bell.

The Commoner slumped to the stool in the blue corner; head both bloody and bowed. His head was so close to his knees that he seemed to be praying; and, indeed he was. Actually, he thought he had "prayed-up" on the way to the studio. He just needed a little help getting inside. All he had planned to do was play the part of the strong silent scholar... ask a question or two... "style and profile" for the camera a little bit... and, at the end of the show rush back to the pool-hall to collect on his bets. While he was making those bets, he had no idea that he would wind up praying, between rounds, for deliverance from the coming rain of rapier like left jabs followed by rapid fire right crosses that would most certainly be aimed at taking his head off. That coming barrage was sure to further impair his ability to think.

Suddenly, as clear as a bell cutting through dense fog, it came home to him what the old folks meant when they said to be careful what you prayed for; and he immediately began to re-word the prayer he was in the midst of composing. Then he stopped to assess whether he should be praying at all. He seemed to remember running across a proverb that said there is a time to pray, and, then again, there is a time to think. Sneaking a quick peek over at the red corner, he could see the panel, as one, licking its chops; – and, suddenly, it came clear to him what was meant by the colloquialism "taking a licking". As though of its own accord, his mind ceased to be double minded and focused in on the coming rain of blows… the coming rain of blows… the coming rain… It was at that point that a thought entered his head and blew the cobwebs completely away: <u>there can be an ocean of water without there being a drop of rain, but there cannot be a single drop of rain without water</u>.

Now he had a game plan. He would rush across the ring, go into a clinch, and offer to throw the fight — on one condition. No doubt they would let him know very quickly that they would accept nothing less than total and unconditional surrender; and, while they were doing so, he would bet them that they didn't know the difference between water and rain. He knew that intellects loved riddles. Nothing would give them greater pleasure than to solve his riddle – and then knock him out.

He knew that it might not take a panel of superior intellects long to see that water is an element and rain is an activity, but, by then, if things went according to plan, he would hit them with the implications of the answer… if it was correct. If the answer were not correct, or if they failed to come up with an answer, he would supply them with one. He was mildly surprised when no answer was forthcoming, but he was not surprised at all that there was no admission by any member that he did not know the answer. More importantly, not a single jab had been thrown.

Before they could collect themselves and get back to the matter of his credentials, he quickly stepped in with the explanation that rain is a weather/gravity related activity, totally dependent on the availability of water, while, on the other hand, water is an element that need not fall from clouds to be what it is. For there to be rain, water must be part of the equation; but, for water to be water, rain is not a necessity.

While they were absorbing what they undoubtedly would dismiss as frivolous irrelevance, he jabbed them (bip bip) with the proposition that there was a similar relationship between thought and a thinking. As rain is a dependent activity, so is thinking a dependent activity. As water is an independent physical reality, so is thought an independent metaphysical reality. Rain depends on water, thinking depends on thought. (bip bip).

Moreover, just as water is water whether it is raining or not, so is thought going to remain thought whether he, they, unidentified flying and creeping aliens, or anyone else in the universe was thinking or not thinking… and, whether he, or they, or any of the others had their "own truth" or not. Even if the activity of thinking were not presently present anywhere in a "moment of silence" universe, thought would <u>not</u> be momentarily absent anywhere in the universe. A fishing reel is real even if the line is <u>never</u> unreeled. He was not trying to draw blood because he didn't like the sight of it, but that shot still was a (bop).

Like the "now", thought is not dependent upon, or subject to, anyone or anything. Even when it is the subject of debate, it does not lose any of its objectivity. Consequently, not one itty- bitty little bit of thinking can be engaged in that does not automatically presuppose the immutable, presently-present, absolute, objective reality of thought. They might refute him and his lack of credentials, but they could not refute that. As a matter of fact, he would still keep his part of the bargain they had refused to enter into, and throw the fight – on one condition. They would have to find a way to convey their wish for him to do so without resorting to thought.

He didn't have to throw the (bam!).

Needless to say, that was the "fittest" end to the championship reign of an "idea whose time has come". For quite awhile, that idea gave the appearance of having evolved into a global tsunami, but all along, in reality, that reign had been much weaker than a puddle of primordial water. Just like that, the champs of the IQ elite had been blown out of the water and into a contest with the rule of elasticity that is innate in the "blown-up" aspect of the law of gravity. Up, up and away they had been blown; until the gravity of the situation had "had it up to here" with the chaotic revolutions of that kind of nonsense. The observable reality, at the apogee of that high-flying lie, was the loop around into the downpour… raining itty-bitty chunks of one panel full of itty-bitty chumps. And just like that, champ to chump, the time for that particular, peculiar, "idea whose time had come"… was gone.

XXXXXXXXXXX

With the tail pinned firmly on the donkey, it would seem that the fight would be all over. And, that would be a reasonable assumption for one who does not know the fiesty, yeasty, nature of those chunky little chumps. But, with that ology/ism ilk, "when the fat lady sings", it is time to repair to the back room and check to see if the little rods of stainless steel in their ball point pens are full of ink before beginning the process of loophole reparations that will restore them to their thrones on august panels. One thing that would be immediately obvious to the little chumps is that when the home field advantage has been lost; and when the game is no longer being played at a home base which is not yet highly evolved enough to chance touching base with anything absolute; — like rigor mortis, disillusionment begins to set in rather quickly.

Clearly, they would have little choice but to begin to see that an even playing field encourages prevailing winds to blow the cloud cover off of the ambiguous sets of rules favored by those used to dictating terms, — and that would be disillusioning. And they would begin to see that their highly evolved rule of thumb; (Since all is illusion… if it feels good, do it), would no longer apply; — as there just is not a whole lot that feels good to the terminally ill. On the darker side of those deliberations, it would begin to sink in, that what had been bad for the evolutionological cooked goose was probably going to be just as bad for the transmigration of its soul into the projected evolutionogistic gander.

They may have been knocked out, but it is far too early for such a unique species to be counted out. They may appear to be just a portly line up of washed up, anachronistic Humpty Dumptys, but it is not for nothing that they are not alone in seeing themselves as great men. Not just any bunch of ordinary champs can reap undeclared global profits made trafficking in cooked-up pseudoscientific textbooks sold on the cornered marketplace that is sometimes referred to as the global village — not without attracting the attention of the IRS. That is no small feat.

What has to be kept in mind is that the IRS has cooked up an anti-cooked-book set of volumes of books that are chock full of rules with loopholes that can make that which is certifiably squeaky clean look like the gate of hell, and make that which is certifiably a gate to hell look like it is squeaky clean; — depending on what has been pragmatically predetermined as fit to survive. Those volumes of heavily sedated semantics allow the IRS to tolerate well executed billion dollar tricks, while, at the same time, with SWAT teams for back-up, it does not miss a trick when it comes to collecting its proper percentage of an itty-bitty fast-food tip.

The fact that certain of the empaneled, elite, core of stipend hounds are totally exempt from purse-string scrutiny is a tribute to just how much clout they wield. And, you just have to give it to a bunch of guys who, after all they have been knocked out of, are resilient enough to take a cooked goose and grate on its transmigrating soul in an attempt to make a gander that will produce goslings. That kind of grating, alone, is enough to show how great they are.

As great as they are, even those dethroned champs have to be asking themselves just how much of a game can there be left to star in when merely stepping up to the plate to assume a hitter's stance is the logical equivalent of a genuflection to the declaration that "thought" is, absolutely, an objective reality. Trying to think of a way to think – without resorting to that, seemingly, ubiquitous imperative – is like trying to hit a home-run without a bat. Come to think of it, not even a bunt can be laid down without a bat. Without a bat, there is no way to get to first base, let alone second or third. Without a bat, it's not even possible to get a walk (except back to the dugout), because the pitcher is not allowed to pitch to a hitter without a bat. To heavy hitters used to a certain percentage of "off-the-top" "home-frees" being already in the bag before the national anthem is played, being without a bat is heavy disillusionment.

Yet, without going forth and assuming the batter's stance and praying –oops… hoping for a miracle… grasping for some sort of miraculous straw… the chances of ever getting around the bases to return to home plate are absolutely nil. Though the evolutionary base has been thoroughly discredited, that is to say; that slate has been swept clean, it cannot be abandoned. It might seem unreasonable, but the reason it simply cannot be abandoned is because it is the only home the "fittest" survivors have ever known. Briefly, they toyed with the idea of closing their eyes to the fact that toying with an idea involves "thought", because that would mean taking "thought" for granted. It did not escape them that taking "thought" for granted is the logical equivalent of admitting that "thought" is a given. Naturally, letting one "given" into the equation would mean having to justify why another is not given an equal opportunity. And, before you know it, there goes the whole ballgame. So, being without either an argument or a rebuttal, they had to abandon that idea.

For the sake of argument and domestic tranquility, let's say that a resourceful heavy hitter somehow managed to replicate himself a bat. Though the game is over, he is allowed by the umpire to take a few swings at the fences to show his date sitting in a box seat what he could have done during the game if he had had a bat. However, since one high-tech dating method dated the shell being carried on the back of a living snail at one billion years old, and another high-tech dating method dated the same shell as two billion years old, regardless of the age of the living snail, high-tech has struck out. And, since there are enough strikeouts like that on scientific record to cover a couple of extra inning double-headers, the heavy hitter has already struck out, by proxy, before he ever gets to take a swing with his replicated bat. The heavy hitter, in effect, becomes a carbon-based-eunuch. His date left the box seat after seeing the results of the high-tech dating machines being methodically swept under the slate, -oops- plate, by the umpire. So, being out of dates, it is obvious that the heavy hitter never really had a ghost of a chance of getting to first base in the first place… not even with a bat that had been unreasonably replicated purely for the sake of replicating a reasonable argument. Even with his "own truth", he never had a chance.

Without a doubt, leaving the dugout would have been a complete waste of time if it were not for the fact that, due to the Piltdown meltdown and a dirty laundry list of other proven frauds, the dugout was also getting into the swing of things by rapidly evolving toward the advanced stages of a bad case of sinking-ship disease. Let the record show that the foregoing scenario was only for the sake of argument, and that, since the heavy hitter was batless, it is only logical to assume that there could have been no other way for the batter to be but hitless.

So it would seem that the days are gone when high IQ championship belts can entitle their credentialed holders to kick politically incorrect commonsense notions to the curb without reflecting on the loss of their belts. As hidden scientific artifacts are found and raised from the basements of the museums of the global village, it would seem that making a show of commoners openly, while scorning them into dimwit cells located in the intellectual catacombs, may soon be going the way of the archaeopteryx and the dodo.

The more the theory of evolution is scrutinized, the more it seems likely that, almost from inception, it may have been recognized by quick witted opportunists that even though it was unable to make the cut as science, it might be able to cut the muster as a brave "new truth" whose time has arrived. Those far-seeing intellectual pharisees, seemingly, were able to see that, as a philosophical outlook, that theory could, with intelligent promotion, be evolved into a secular religion which could then be gradually elevated to a substrata of sub-natural divine fact. All it would take would be the judicious superstitching of semantics to bring the concept of your own "new truth" online, and, from there, the sky would be the limit, beyond which no further speculation, after a period of indoctrination, would be allowed.

Almost from its inception, then, it seems that the theory has been a subject without any predicate other than to establish a base in order to home-in on a way to eradicate commonsense by means of cutting down on the growing populations of commoners. Thus, seemingly, it is beginning to appear that the Big Bang designed to support that headless clone of a theory is the sound heard around the global village of the crack of the dinosaur egg omelet exploding off homey's plate — smack dab in the middle of a batless, hitless, heavy hitter's long-wrong face. Seemingly, the pragmatically humanistic, superstitched, chicken-bleep, seamantics have come back to the homo sapiens homey's home plate to, in the vernacular, grab a squat. Seemingly, such sappy soppings would be so yucky that some mouths would need to be washed out with soap.

So, it appears that all the head-scratching, cap straightening, and phantom-bat swinging taking place on the short journey from the dugout to the plate is just a lot of futile posturing. Nothing at, on, or near, the first base side of that particular batter's box is even open to debate; —not to the first baseless, goose egg, foolishness of a batless, de-evolutionized, disillusionary, anyway. And, it is a leadbat cinch that what's going down back at the dugout is still rapidly evolving its way into a face to face encounter with its "own truth"; – which is nothing nice.

Seemingly, pointing out the way off the field, without pointing out the absolute necessity of the preexistence of the field, would be a gracious gesture. Resisting the urge to point out that taking a few tablespoons full of commonsense is really the only way to go would be gracious also. The problem is that the high IQ muckty-mucks have traditionally disdained trafficking with that which is common, and are used to being the dispensers… not the recipients (except from nobles who see to their welfare), and are not likely to appreciate being shown the exit by an inferior, anyway. Gracious gestures, at this point, could be a bit premature, and might, down the road, turn out to be a gross error. Chucked-out chunky chumps, not at all fond of having to say farewell to their welfare checks, are not known in philosophic circles as comeback kids for nothing.

To the ecologically worshipful animal rights advocates (who have it on good authority that mother nature, if she ever had one, has long since, either divorced, or been divorced by, her husbandman), ordering silver bullets and wooden stakes may seem like rubbing it in, or worse; like beating a dead horse. What they fail to understand, (along with the reason why no animal has evolved a language to litigate for their rights themselves), is that this breed of horse has a Dracula type track record of playing possum. This peculiar breed of beast has a very long history of rising from great depths to resurface under the guise of one scholarly sounding ology/ism or another.

No doubt, even as that possum-playing, switch-hitting, panel of semantic superstiching beasts departs from the field, as one highly illumined mind, it is dreaming up a plan that will allow it to keep right on with business as usual just as soon as it can figure out a way to raise its Post Modern oxymoronic head. Despite the regal heights attained by its collective of IQs, it is oblivious to the fact that, if it is "Post", it cannot be "Modern". But, then again, maybe that term is not so oxymoronic after all. It could be that that august group is working out their "own truth" so as to try to postdate a modern check up into the past. Those itty-bitty chumps are sly little devils. Any panel that sly has to be beaten to the punch again and again in order to be convinced that all is not an illusion... that its head does indeed exist; and that it does not exist as a reincarnated mulehead without any "givens" for a clue, either. Clues are all over the place.

Along with the baggage carried by every semantical trick is a bag of clues waiting to point out where evidence of the attempt at "verbicide" may be found. There are even short-sighted clues for the shortsighted. The attempt to murder existance by calling it an illusion is a good example of a shortsighted case which makes that point. The clues in the sandbagging of existance are so upfront that they cannot be missed... only dismissed by being pooh-poohed into insignificance. When "existance" is back-engineered into the two words, "exist" and "stance", those words become dots that call for more dots until there are enough dots to divulge how the dots would have been connected had there been no semantical hanky-panky.

The word "exit" is a "dot" which presupposes that a move has been made from one site to another. That "dot" also presupposes that, even if that prior site was only cited as an instance, it was a position, or location, that was there to be cited. It was a "stance". When that "stance" abandons one place (dot) to move to another place (dot), it has made an "exit" from that abandoned site, or position, to enter into a subsequent "stance". Thus, the prerequisite for the movement out of one stance into another stance was the exit of the prior stance from its prior site. That particular "exit" could only have been made by that particular "stance"... and no other. Therefore, that particular "exit" belongs to that particular "stance"... and no other. That particular "stance" belongs to that particular "exit". As often happens when a two word phrase has been married into one meaning, the tendency is to meld into one term. Thus, the melding of "exit" and "stance" slides easily into existance.

Lest it be thought that the prior exegesis was a word trick, or a stretch, think what might be done with the dots left by "ill", "lucid", and "straight", if they were to be connected as a further il-lu-straition that hanky-panky is extant when attempts are made to foist existance off as an illusion. An exit from any sphere, even the sphere of influence shrouding the batless wonder in the batter's box, might be said to be an ex-sphere-ance. It's a stretch, but not an unwarranted stretch, (especially after witnessing the boot out of the ballpark), to see how such an exit might be thought of as quite an experience. Whether or not that stretch is able to provide the logical closure that would come with a "four-bagger", the fact is, there would not have been any dots to connect had it not been for the clues that, obviously, could hardly wait to come out of a bag. Without them, the exegesis could never have even gotten to first base. The original point, after all, was to demonstrate that such bags of clues exist. And, as far as tricks are concerned, the fact that they must all step up to the plate, eventually, without a bat, is the next point.

At the risk of being hauled off to animal court for desecrating a reincarnated mulehead, it must be pointed out that there is a fundamental difference between a trick and a fraud. To suggest that existance is an illusion is to shroud the real issue in clouds of the kind of frustrating confusion that causes a discussion of origins to be abandoned with the parting shot that it's all just "a matter of semantics", anyway. Then, the question as to whether or not existance could be pre-sent into the present as a gift, issued forth into a "Now" that is being continually sustained, is never even addressed. Shrouding that issuing forth with confusing clouds is the trick.

The presupposition inherent in any present now-moment that is considered to be a gift is that there has to be a giver. A presupposed giver whose face is never seen can be given the "cloud" treatment and pooh-poohed into insignificance while global village business goes on as usual. But the presupposition, which is also inherent in a gift, that is a big problem, is the given. The given comes face to face with the idea that the "present", theoretically, evolved from the primordial pool, which, theoretically, was the product of a Big Bang. When challenged, that Big Bang has the unique ability to call for a pinch hitting theory with the unique ability to call for a pinch hitter with the ability to call for a pinch hitter with the ability to call for a pinch hitter with the ability to call for a pinch hitter with the ability to call… and so on and on, theoretically, "for millions and millions of years". That way, with a giver-less gift, the batless batter can continue to reign as the hitless home run king, for millions and millions of years, also. The endless regression of pinch hitters is another trick. The batless batter is the fraud.

It seems, then, that existance was called into question for the unstated purpose of shrouding it in enough clouds to confuse the issue enough for it to serve as a smokescreen. In the confusion, that smokescreen could be used to divorce the reason for the existance of reason from any kind of reasonable explanation; and then, while the unexplained was being used as a decoy, the smokescreen could be extended to cloak the dagger being stuck in the back of commonsense in order to provide the free hand needed by highly illumined itty-bitty chumps to "run it" the way their welfare nobility sees "fittest".

Though there has been plenty of blood and guts to tolerate, the majority of the damage was done on the playing fields of pragmatic semantics. By mixing sense with nonsense, your "own truth" with other's "own truth", the "which is witch" brew could be baited and switched from the cauldron of half-truths disseminated in cases of what might, at first glance, appear to be six six six packs of whole lies. Fortunately, since the lie depends on truth being twisted and bent into a lie for its existance, there is no such thing as a whole lie. Providentially, the letter of the linguistic law does not have to be hewn out of stone for it to spear it a lie right in its lying bullseye. (Witness the metaphysical spearhead buried in the chest full of mulehead lies.)

As much as it hates to contemplate origins, let alone deal with them, even a mulehead cannot avoid seeing, try as it might, something ominous in what appears to be a semantical boomerang that is both primal and lethal. But a mule-head would have to be hogtied and de-programmed to admit that, while belief in something like semantical life might be a stretch, it is nowhere near the stretch it takes to believe in the evolution-inspired high wire act featuring the tap dance of the "free floating means"... always at the ready to support any pragmatic end that seems to be able to make a contribution toward the survival of the "fittest".

Hypothetically, an "all middle – no end" philosophical stunt like that is the logical equivalent of antigravitational antimatter. In layman's terms, the theory of evolution, as foisted, is a secular religious philosophy, masquerading as science, whose foundational premise is a levitating question that depends on the lack of a plausible answer to continue levitating. The solution to that kind of theoretical nonsense is to leave both the theory and the theorists suspended where they are... over a black hole that, it is written, is the habitat "where their worm dieth not".

Less easily seen (because of the smokescreen), but far more compelling than even the ominous u-turn-ings of semantical boomerangs is the fact that implicit in the seminal meaning of the word existance is the presupposition of a preexistant state. (Nonsense could not have been kicked out of the ballpark had there been no preexistant park to be kicked out of.) So, even if the panel had been successful in aborting the child (existance) by smokescreening it completely out of the picture, it then would have had to fast forward the evolution of a herculean fire extinguisher in order to deal with the approach of the parent (BEING), which the seeming success of the removal of existance would have revealed. The only possible outcome of such seam-antics would be a face to face encounter with the universal steed of BEING upon which the truth rides. The bad news would be that preexistant purity and subsequent impurity cannot ride the same horse. The worse news is that the u-turns of the boomerangs are designed to make sure that that is one seam-antic that does not even get tried. Obviously, the boomerangs would have to be bridled before attempting to deal with anything else.

But the highly-illumined panel of chummy chumps couldn't even put a bridle on the little pony "existance", because, like Cain, it was not able.

XXXXXXXXX

The domains of existance are usually limited, by mule-heads, to those things which can be seen by the physical eye. Things which cannot be seen, such as “choice”, “time”, and “chance” are considered to be the natural by-products of the evolution of the brain. Thus, the human brain, with its intellectual prowess, is thought to be positioned at the apex of all that is. Any territory “all that is” does not yet cover is just there waiting to be conquered by the further evolution of the brain, which, of course, is encased inside the heads of a bunch of really smart cookies… humans. Therefore, the brave new order of the fast coming new age is “Humanism… the pragmatic school, of course.

The physical, the actual, and the tangible, are considered to be the inhabitants of the only state that is real. The metaphysical, the mystical, the ethereal, are considered to be irrelevant, surreal, states of mind that touch base with reality from time to time, like spectral images often seen in dissipating clouds. They belong to the world of illusion which is the ethereal preamble to nothingness. However, the word “ethereal” has been semantically neutered to conjure up thoughts of an abnormal otherworldliness that shares borders with the world of hallucinations. Since "ethereal" has the word "real" in it, it would seem that (were it not for the antics) it would have something to do with something that is real.

The ethereal is not limited to being stuck in the physical domain where all that is is bound by its form. It seems obvious that it was because of its ' ' freedom from bondage that the ethereal quality came to be described as "miss-stick-l". That which is mystical is free to enter the state of wholeness to be found only in the timeless union of reality with BEING. So, no view can be farther from the truth than the one that idolizes the physical domain as the end all and be all of reality. That time bound, existential, outlook is destined to be blown out of the cosmic exhaust pipe along with the rest of the nonsense and foolishness disappearing into the abyss that is devoid of BEING.

BEING is the changeless realm of reality which is the abode of ideals like truth, thought… even life itself… from which existance made its exit. In that realm, natural law and relative terms, though not violated, are supernaturally superceded and do not apply. That realm is changless because nothing dwells there that is not equally as perfect as it is ideal. As any pear on a pear tree is as much pear as any other, everything that is true of one facet of BEING is equally, and simultaneously, just as true of any and all others. The standard measure for anything that dwells in that realm is that it be infinitely beyond measure. In that regard, truth, thought, and even love are changelessly indistinguishable, one from the other. And, if it were possible to find a reason to change that which is perfection itself, what need could there possibly be to change that which can be neither more nor less than what it already is or is ever going to be? BEING has no nature because it is the supernatural sustainer of nature. Its utter perfection is immutable.

Because BEING is changeless it is also ageless. As a matter of fact, it encompasses time, the progenitor of aging, as the ocean encompasses a bubble. (Strictly speaking, existance is an internal secretion). Only forms which exist inside the bubble of time are subject to, or affected by, the aging process. And, it is only from the process of change that the concept of beginnings and endings can arise. Unless there is a procession from a beginning toward an ending, the concept of aging does not apply, and will not compute. In time, or out of time, "Now" is always now. There simply isn't anything to compute. In like manner, "thought", (as opposed to the thinking process), is not a process, but an ideal. It has no beginning or ending any more than perfection itself does. Outside of existance, not only is time not observed, it is not relevant. The ethereal reality of BEING is timeless.

In the ethereal light of the forgoing, it would seem that all the vast distances of incomprehensible infinity, in order to be imagined, must be conceptualized in terms of that which may be comprehended… the finite. Distances, no matter how vast, in order to be measured, must either come to an end, or be arbitrarily assigned an end. It just is not possible to say how long a journey has been, or how much time it has taken, until that journey has been completed. Since distance and time are not factors that can be factored into BEING, whatever their measure may be calculated to be will be the answer to a question that cannot be anything other than moot.

So, all beginnings and endings are limited to the distances between forms, and the spans of the lives of forms, that are governed by the innate rhythmic tours of cycles and seasons of the natural world. Since both the infinite and the infinitesimal are encompassed by BEING, in order for BEING to have had a beginning, a way would have had to have been found for BEING to be contained by a finite existance which is wholly encompassed by BEING. In natural terms, in the natural scheme of natural relationships and natural laws, such a feat would be the logical equivalent of a Godzillian type camel being swallowed by a gnat.

Obviously then, until that particular gnat swallows that particular camel in its entirety, for BEING, clearly, there just cannot be any such thing as an end. So it only stands to reason (to the reasonable) that, though distance, aging, and time, all of which have a beginning; are affected by BEING, they, in turn, have less effect on BEING than a cup of ice water can have on putting an end to a forest fire.

Paradoxically, what boggles the mind is that, for all its mind-blowing potency, BEING doesn't seem to be doing anything. The fact is, though BEING does not act, its perfection is such that, without acting, it does everything that is done. Its potency is such that it needs only to be, for all that there is, to be. Speaking of paradox, at the same time that BEING is more macrocosmically distant than the outermost speck of cosmic dust, it is also more microcosmically immediate than a strand of DNA. Everywhere present, the cosmic paradox is, being everywhere, its own resolution, and that means that it has to also be the cosmic equator… or equinox. It is the All in all that really is – which, of course, includes mulehead illusions out.

BEING, the All in all, is so inclusive that it includes even the abominable mulehead, out of which those illusions proceed; — the mulehead that it cannot abide and does not pervade, which is, itself, only two minutes away from being included out eternally. BEING is so singular that all that it includes that is not a "plus" is a "positive". It knows nothing of negation because it cannot suffer a minus, (which is an imperfection), to escape being quarantined, in its own quarters, in a domain of existance. In BEING, what may appear to be opposite extremes which are poles apart, are really complementary components that function together as one whole.

Since any duality that does not function harmoniously is included out, BEING has no opposition that is not blinded to the futility of attempting to oppose a cosmic principality that cannot be opposed – because it cannot be invaded by that which it does not pervade. On the other hand, that which it does pervade cannot oppose BEING because it is a part of the composition of that which cannot be opposed. Moreover, BEING, the All in all, is such a singularity that it cannot be altered to become otherwise for the simple reason that, by including all that really is, there really isn't a single thing that can escape the principle of singularity to perform the alteration… without quenching itself in the very act of attempting to escape. Of such is the oneness of BEING.

It is an understatement to say that understanding even a few anthills in the foothills of the mountain ranges of

BEING is awesome, astonishing, and astounding. In trying to figure out a way to visualize BEING, the analogy of "a universal womb without walls" raises more questions than it answers because its walls are what makes a womb; so, the metaphor is useless except as a starting point for beginning to realize how much is not known about how boggled a mind can become. An effort to see BEING as the foundation of all foundations would prove to be shortsighted, also. When a little thought is given the matter, BEING would have to be seen as being beyond being merely foundational... as foundations may be undermined, overruled, overwhelmed, or confounded. It would have to be seen as being beyond being merely elemental, as well, because, in their innate tours, elements may cast shadows, and they may react to cold or heat. BEING does not react to anything at all. Just as it does not act, neither does it react.

It, would seem to be inescapable, then, that, if it is not the dwelling place of the origin of all origins which is, itself, without an origin, BEING cannot be far from whatever is. However much more it may or may not be, BEING can be no less, for "existance", than a ubiquitous imperative which is so self-luminous that it needs no apologists. Without a single utterance, it speaks all the uncontestable volumes necessary for it to be its own self-authenticating course of study in apologetics. Yet, the enormity of the magnitude of the significance of whatever might be contained in those volumes may be understood by the realization of the magnificence comprehended by a single word – that word being – BEING.

XXXXXXXX

At this stage of a game that really has been over for a very long time, it would seem that the only way remaining to evolve a case for "existance" being an illusion would be to try as hard as possible to suppress any idea of trying to think of a way to try to evolve a case. Even a switch from trying to impress to trying to suppress won't make a difference, because no try, one way or the other, can be attempted without BEING. Either way they go, skeptics are trapped.

But, entrapment is not necessarily a bad thing (as in the case of an injured animal who must be trapped to be treated), and neither is every skeptic necessarily a bad guy.

Believing their professors, some were simply repelled by what they were indoctrinated into perceiving to be the foolishness of religious and semi-religious myths and lies. They had been sidetracked into the victimization of the "end justifies the means" methodology mainstreamed into the New Age new breed of "science with an attitude" foisted upon them by instructors who, themselves, more than likely, had been victimized. Some who set out, like outraged crusaders, to debunk, once and for all, what they perceived to be pernicious "opiate of masses" impediments, upon rigorously investigating the facts, have come to be numbered among the most eloquent defenders of the veracity of that which they had set out to debunk. So, there is no hard and fast rule that a skeptic must evolve into a mulehead skoffer. For skeptics who strictly adhere to scientific methodology, entrapment means deliverance. For all others it means playing possum.

Due to their muleheadness, needless to say, scoffers remain trapped. But, just because they are trapped does not mean the little litter of trumped chumps have given up the ghost. Though they can hardly bear the thought of hibernation, they will not hesitate to do so if they think they can form a think tank in hopes of dreaming up a Post-Post Modern primordial pool of supercharged, space-age, pragmatic, humanism super-attenuated enough to allow them to search for a seam in the logic of a BEING whose logic is, apparently, seamless. So: Yes…

> (Actually, when a trumped-up theory like evolution has been so thoroughly demolished that any attempt to defend it proves that it is indefensible, the seamlessness of the demolishing logic is not merely apparent; it is so conclusive that it makes any attempt at defense as retroactively ridiculous as a propaganda barrel full of monkey trial-balloon movies. There isn't enough of that theory left for the wind to inherit.

Can't be… it transmigrated into a proposition that is wholly hoax.)

Virginia, as hard as it might be for a rational mind to believe, there is a species of batless clean slate advocates who, though aware of the illusionary aspects of the party line, are willing to evolve along with the unraveling hoax purely as a matter of mulehead choice.

The difference between regular "choice" and mulehead "choice" (unless muleheads re-pen the lies written in the textbooks mandated throughout the global village and lose a lot of muleface in the process) is that muleheads have no choice but to keep on being muleheads for as long as they keep on playing possum. Without entering the hypothetical, bewitching, forest of "choice" for fear of becoming enchanted by its ethereal beauty, on one hand, or of getting in too deep to see the forest for the trees, on the other, and losing sight of the task at hand, observations will be made from its periphery. The task is to examine the roots of the illness of logic as it is manifested in the twisted and truncated branchings of trees irregularly pruned by muleheads.

Ideally, "choice" is the right and ability to branch off in any direction that limbs appear to be laden with the most desirable fruit. However, even when it seems that the choice could not be more clear, there is the potential for selecting a limb bearing fruit that is less than the best. So, intrinsic in any fork-in-the-road duality, there is "choice". But, when semantical obfuscation fogs the leaves of a tree in shrouding clouds, some of its limbs are, in effect, sawed off. For all practical purposes, that kind of monkey business turns what used to be a branch into a stump. "Choice" is narrowed.

The stunting of physical growth is an anatomical process that can be seen with the physical eye. Stumping mental maturation (dumbing down), however, is an axiomatic process. The results are not so easily seen because the amount of damage done depends on what axioms have been instilled in the mind, and, to what degree a mind adheres to that which has been instilled. Without having to be a rocket scientist, what is known is that every limb-probing excursion must either lead to fruit or to a stump… to regeneration or to degeneration.

It is also known that three things are essential to making a choice. There must be something to choose, the will to choose, and the freedom to exercise the will. Commonsense tells anyone willing to listen that tampering with any one of those essentials cannot help but have an adverse effect on the other two. If a branch has been fogged, the will has to be unsure; and the outcome of a decision will be "iffy". If a decision is forced upon a will that is not free, no choice has been made, because that is coercion. When fed misinformation and/or disinformation, the will that seems to function as though it were free has really been compromised.

Obviously, then, distortion, compounded by interaction with the distortion that is already extant, cannot help but to exponentially increase the clouds of confusion that are the standard foggy fare on the tollway to degeneration which is well traveled by the "survival of the fittest" muleheads who are just barely "hanging-in". Just as obvious, is the fact that, given a choice between lying and coming clean, the possum-playing mulehead would rather continue to lie there dreaming up schemes of ways to capitalize on the confiscation of other people's "choice".

No doubt, the love of occupying elevated positions, where lying for fun and profit is the order of the day, is one reason why muleheads never bothered to dispute the theory that the appearance of life on the planet, "millions and millions of years ago", is explained by the formula: "With time... by chance... through evolution". Aside from totally ignoring the fact that there must have been an author of the cookbook containing the recipe for primordial soup, the most obvious flaw in the thinking of whoever cooked up that primordial dish is the inclusion of that most ephemeral of ingredients called "time".

Time did not back then... does not now... and never will in the future be able to stop to become an ingredient. Oh, it can stop alright – stop on a dime. That's what a stop-watch is for; and that's why a one hour sporting event, with commercial breaks, can take three hours to complete. But, whenever time stops, it has no time to be, or to become, an ingredient, or anything else, because it vanishes immediately; and that particular span of time is no more. (A time span is like a fingerprint – everything has its own.)

Time is not an entity. It is an abstract tool of measure extrapolated from the cyclical movement of two celestial entities… the earth's tours around the sun. In order for the measures to be taken, markings were made where shadows fell. From those humble beginnings, the markings evolved into the sundial, which, eventually evolved into the clock. The clock is a mechanized extrapolation, inspired by a shadowy abstraction, that is still no more, and no less, than a representation of a cycle around the sun. Its face has been drawn, quartered, and calibrated to synchronize the activities, more or less, of the planet. It will come as a surprise to some that time has never healed a single wound. The only thing it can do is measure how long it takes a wound to heal. To some, the concept of "time" may have begun to appear to be a human invention. It is.

It is never going to evolve into being able to transmigrate into evolving, because it is strictly dependent on the spans of that which is measured for its existance. When any one of those spans expires, its "time" expires along with it. Even the overarching span, from its beginning to now, expires, and is constantly expiring, now, at the doorway to the timelessness of BEING. Since nothing in BEING is subject to time, for all practical purposes, time vanishes there.

As a factor in the formula for evolution, "time" has many flaws; — not the least of which is, that, in order for the theory to hold up, "time"... the invention... would have had to predate its inventer. Besides being inherently preposterous, that "hind parts before" proposition is an instance of one time when "time" just does not fly. So, unless its inventer is "millions and millions of years" old, for that kind of "millions and millions of years" foolishness, time is out. That means that the whole evolutionary load has to be carried by "chance" if the theory is to survive.

One problem with "chance" having to bear the load alone is that, from its inception, it had even less of a chance of surviving than "time". Like "time", it is not an entity. It depends on "choice" for its existance. It depends on there being a branching-off… a fork in the road. Where there is no choice to be made, there is no chance of "chance" even having an inception, because, without "choice", "chance" is so far out of the question it cannot even be a question that is moot.

The very existance of "chance" presupposes that, somewhere along the road, someone has barked up the wrong tree, or branched off in the wrong direction by making a choice that was less than ideal. That is the only way that "chance" could get into the picture. So "choice" and "chance" are joined at the hip… two sides of the same coin. "Choice" is heads… "chance" is tails. To take a choice is to make a decision. Taking a chance is risky business… a toss up… a roll of the dice. "Chance" is the stuff of which naturally selected mutations are made. The upshot is, since "chance" is dependent on "choice" for its existance, it is not primary, but secondary, and, as such, has no business in a formula of primal beginnings, anyway.

That little upshot is only one of its downfalls. The big problem is that "time" has already been canceled out of the equation. Without "time", the window of opportunity for natural selection to get on with any mutation it might make goes out the window. There just wouldn't be time for a single roll of the dice, or even one toss-up. Where there is no "time" for a "chance", there simply cannot be any chance at all of evolving a naturally selected mutation to make even a shot-in-the-dark change. So, with the implosion of the formula, the question becomes: what are the chances that the theory will be found fit enough to survive? With a vanquished formula that imploded and vanished from the environs of the primordial pool, the answer is obvious. Not a chance.

Because it thinks it sees a semantical chink in the anti-evolution argument that it might be able to exploit, the mule-head eye blinks. What it thinks it sees is a chance to seize another "chance" by changing its time-bound terminology to "seasons" and "cycles" and, by doing so, redeem the vanished "time". That redemption, alone, would supply it with a "chance" to plug into a rejuvenated formula. In this technological age, it wouldn't have to have a whole new primordial pool to supply it with slime. A single drop of rain, bearing a single simple cell, is all it would take to get the evolution show back on the road. Being a sadder and wiser old mulehead, it continued to play possum so as not to let on that it had seen the chink. At the right time, it would spring forth with a brave new idea which would be irresistible because its "time" had re-arrived. Visions of think tank poshness were interspersed with its scheming dreams.

The mulehead would do well to dream on, and forget that scheme, because there isn't a single simple cell on the whole planet. There are more molecule sized machines in a single cell than all the factories on the planet put together. Moreover, they are all systemically interconnected so that if a part of one system fails, the cell dies. The complexity in a single cell is so mind boggling that it well may be that the universal macrocosm has been replicated in the microcosm. The myriad of interconnections of the internet, by comparison, are probably less complex than a spider web. Such complexity makes the question of intelligent design moot... to anyone but a mulehead clamped down and padlocked in a stock... on display in a way that gives new meaning to the term laughingstock. Still in tact is the zero "chance" and zero "time" which add up to be the Post Modern mother of all the goose eggs — overseen and superintended by the muleheads — with their large cranial capacities crammed full of the primordial slime that, judging by the goose eggs, is just not fit to survive.

The mystery is how such an asinine theory could come to be taught in schools in every nook and cranny of the global village. The atrocity is that the indoctrinated answers had better be forthcoming, or there will be failing grades and ridicule on the kindergarten level, and denial of tenure and loss of livelihood at the Ivory Tower level. The day will come (and now is) when babies, soon after they learn how to say goo-goo, will be taught to say gook! Gook! – phooey on all that brand of new world order mess of potty-pottage. Save it for the feedbags of muleheads who don't see that the law of entropy, while allowing for potty-pottage to be turned into fossilized rock, does not allow that rock to hang a u-turn, and, over "millions and millions of years", contribute the chemicals to a primordial pool that are necessary to evolve into a mulehead.

This is not to say that evolution does not exist; only that it does not exist as it has been palmed off on unsuspecting generations. The comedic possibilities of the theory itself, as well as the possibilities inherent in it being logically extended all the way back to its origins, and the wealth of humorous corollaries inherent in that extension, have only just begun to evolve as the whole cockamamie scheme begins to unravel. Even as a tiny nut (actually a cone seed) evolves into a giant sequoia, Humanistic nuts (actually cone-heads) evolve toward reaching the heights of insanity. Both of those species, the seed and nuts, are the culmination of the growth of organized aggregations of highly specialized cells; but, for lack of the capacity to do so, only one of those species ever evolves to reach the pinnacle of specialization necessary to avail itself of a cell that has been padded.

It is, however, prudent for the prudent never to say never. So, it cannot be dogmatically stated, especially with the rapid scientific advances, that genetic engineering will never evolve to the point where both the flower shop and the pet shop will stock Sechiquoihuahuas ... a new species of genetically engineered dogwood treedog. But that happenstance is not one that even an "on and off" member of gamblers anonymous would characterize as a good bet. By the time the potty pottage crowd begins to potty train their progeny, the very idea that grown men could be mulehead enough to concoct a worldwide educational system, impenetrably full of complex intellectual contortions specifically designed to be a roadblock to any idea seeking to join with any absolute, will have made the mulehead the butt of many a joke. By the time the game of pinning the tail on the donkey evolves to the point of being correlated with the business of pinning primordial tales on muleheads, the numb skull of the possum-player will have already been picked clean, to the bonehead, of any material funny enough to fetch any more of the kind of laughter that induces thighs to be slapped. Or, then again, with the precocious Post New Age breed of early blooming comedians (who are thoroughly grounded in the uncontestable logic inherent in the ubiquitous nature of the imperative innate in BEING) the jokes might go on "for millions and millions of years". A possum-playing mulehead is extremely fertile ground for pooling resources to evolve a myriad of primordial tales to pin on that joker's butt.

XXXXXXXXX

Here again, the focus is not on origins. In following logic's lead, it is inevitable and unavoidable that some issues, which cannot be entirely skirted due to the nature of logic, will be touched upon from time to time. Inferences that stand, like doormen waiting to show the way to ultimate causes, will not be drawn for fear that the discussion will ascend up into a web-work of doctrinal speculations. Attention will be given to the dots themselves; not to connecting them. Like archeological stones anxious to cry out, some dots will cry out to be connected, but, as much possible, those crys will be ignored. The aim will be to attempt to discriminate between the logical and the scatological, as one relates to BEING and the other seeks to disregard it.

Since words are composed of letters, letters are the logical place to begin. Letters are enablers. Like individual links allow chains to be made, depending on how they are arranged, letters "let" a specified meaning into a word. To be more precise, what is meant depends on how the letters are arranged, and, how the letters are arranged depends on what meaning is to be conveyed. Though words are generally taken for granted, there is something magical, mystical, and amazing about the mutual agreement intrinsic in the symbiotic relationship between a thought and its symbolic representation. That "something", partially, is the seamless sealing-in of a designated bit of truth. Ideally, a single word cannot lie because its very composition presupposes agreement on what is meant by whatever is packaged into that spelling.

There are letters that sound exactly like words, "I" and "eye" sound like "aye"; and "b" sounds the same as "be" and "bee". But it would be a digression to pursue the sounds of letters when it is their order and arrangement that is the heart of the discussion. So, where order is concerned, just as a preexistent alphabetical order is a prerequisite for the letting of a specific letter to do a specific letting, so does that letting presuppose that a presumption has been made that there is power in the ordering of letters to do a job. In other words, just as a preestablished monetary system is a prerequisite for selecting a specific number of dollar bills to pay for a hamburger, so does that number of bills presuppose the presumption that there is enough buying power in those bills to pay for the sandwich. If the letter "a" is used to represent that which is preexistent and presupposed, and the letter "b" is used to represent that which exists… that which can be verified by one or more of the five senses, then a+b=c. With the "c" being equal to "see", what would be seen is that the unseen, plus the seen, has to be seen in order for "c" to equal reality. (All that really says is that, seen and unseen, what is… is.)

However, the preexistance issue, along with all of its theological ramifications, will be skirted in order to deal with that which may be apprehended by the five senses, which, in some scientific circles, is considered to be the only logical way to go. Yet, when "a" is skirted to avoid theological tainting, commonsense dictates that the formula is reduced to b=c. According to that truncated rendering, "b"-ing is equated with "c" ing. (Being is the same as seeing).

Commonsense also tells us that one first must "be" before any seeing is possible, and that one can be blind... totally unable to see... and still "be". If that is the case, logic tells us that in no way, in that particular truncation, can b=c. From that particular tarmac, "c"-ing just will not "b" leaving. It is at this point that what commonsense has been telling anyone willing to listen becomes starkly clear: that is one version of logic which is decidedly ill.

When b=c, "be" is said to be equal to "see", and seeing is said to be believing; — even though that which is most real cannot be seen with a set of stereoscopic eyes. As that version of logic evolves, what may be seen snaking its way into the scenario is a sea of seams at the ready to be pried apart and semantically seeded with the pride in a self-esteem that results from seeming to be equal to that which is entirely out of the range of its truncated tunnel vision. Put another way: There is a fleet of boatloads of mulehead tricks tied into doctrines at the ready to be sewn into pried-apart skull seams; — there to be implanted with all the indoctrination necessary to insure that the "fittest" cannot be seen for what they are… an atavistic bunch of anachronistic muleheads… too proud to deal with reality.

Though it may have seemed like the above was a cheap shot set up merely to show-off on a scapegoat, some of it was really just a little kick at a mulehead pretending to be a deadhead and wishing it could be a roadblock. And some of it was an attempt to illustrate the fact that similar sounding words mean that there is more to them than just the letters that meet the eye; — just like there is more menace in a mulehead playing dead than animal rights activists are able to see. And some of the above is supposed to illustrate the fact that, no matter how words are spelled, if their sounds are similar, somehow, someway, there is a natural alliance between them to get to the bottom of a meaning.

Who could argue against the proposition that what meets the eye, (even when it's a nay), in some form or fashion, is also an “aye”, because it must answer “aye” to having met the eye. The citing of the fact that it was the eye that saw the sighting is what makes sense come into the matching of the eye with an aye. In order to see both the upside and the downside in what “aye” saw, it has to be seen that the upside is the power in the letters that spell meaning into words, while the downside is, of course, the evolution of the predatory seamantics boomeranging back at possum-playing muleheads, who, in a heartbeat, blinks “see” into “saw”.

It is quite a coincidence that the seminal formula a+b=c parallels the Alpha Imperative plus the Universal Imperative... the sum of existance. Though the Alpha Imperative “a” cannot be seen with the eye, its presence has to be inferred, if for no other reason than the fact that there is an eye to see that “a” cannot be seen. That eye owes its existance to the Universal Imperative “b”. Thus, the seminal formula parallels the reality that was before there ever was an alphabet to lend form to the formula.

Logic demands that there be a pre-position before any position can be assumed. No pose can be assumed unless there is something to assume it, and a place for that something to assume its position. (If an end run were not being made around theological issues, that would mean that the mere presence of an observable entity would presuppose that it had been pre-sent into the present by someone other than an observable mulehead.) Pre-position = posture (postulation), "a" + "be" = "see" — the posture whose form parallels the formula a+b=c?

That parallel is also in parallel with the paired eyes which may, or may not, be fit enough to see the triune pattern those parallels fit into so neatly. But one thing is for sure, the coinciding of those fittings can hardly be called accidental by any scientist who wishes to be taken seriously. It follows, then, that those Big Bang "survival of the fittest" muleheads just cannot be serious.

Though the logic of alphabetical order seems to demand that what is symbolized by "a" should be explored before exploring the significance of what is symbolized by "b", that demand will be ignored. The Universal Imperative, which, from now on will be represented by BE, cannot be assigned a location because it is not a thing. It is emptiness. Emptiness is not "nothing". It is potential. No full cup can be filled because it lost that potential when it was filled. On the other hand, BE, which has the potential to be anything that can be, is infinite in its potential. Moreover, without BE, fullness would be stymied, frustrated, dammed... because fullness would be potency without any potential. A well full of water cannot fill a cup that is already full.

As a hub, BE is the emptiness that is a receptacle for an axle, and, it is also the waist of the hourglass through which the sand must flow in order to tell time. It is the portal through which potency must flow in order to begin any beginning. BE is the word that also functions as the "letter"... as the enabler.

BE, like emptiness, does not move, but it does continue to be. The axle does not have to move in order for the wheel to roll – it only has to continue to be an axle. So, ironically, while BE still continues to be the same BE that is always was, it is that continuation which logically extends BE into BEING. If BEING, itself, is not the Ubiquitous Imperative;

— as far as existance is concerned, it might as well be; – because, without it, no light could have been let (sent) to be the cause of perfection being begotten in order to avail itself of the power that abides in BEING to, apparently, proliferate perfection.

Power, truth, light, and light, could be thought of as quadrants in that sphere of perfection except for the fact that there is no division in that realm, and since every aspect of it is equally present everywhere in it, there can be no such thing as a quadrant. Those aspects presuppose consciousness, intelligence, and will. And, the mere presence of existance presupposes all those aspects… and more. In one sense, aspects of BEING are like facets of a gemstone. In another sense, they are like windows of opportunity – all of which are accessible to the degree that there is a desire to do so. The windows themselves, however, are beyond degree, because they are openings to a perfection that, in effect, is the universal decree that, in the final analysis, is really not even a sphere. Reality is unbound, and, therefore, has no borders to envelope a sphere.

Obviously, it may be inferred that, in such a realm, the presence of one aspect of BEING does not preclude the simultaneous presence of any other. Love, truth and power, (as opposed to force), and all else that abides in that ideal realm; though all may be manifested differently, in essence they are not different. As is the case in any state of perfection, where nothing can be added and nothing can be subtracted, there is no such thing as relativity. Perfection and relativity are mutually excluding terms. Perfection and objective reality are inextricable. Any observable and repeatable experimental attempt to extricate one from the other will result in the observable and repeated failure of one attempt after another. Both objective reality and perfection are mutually exclusive of relativity. Nothing is, or can be, relativity perfect. Logically, thought, being an objective reality, cannot be subject to the restrictive nature of relativity. It is just as logical that thinking, an activity which begins and ends, cannot be anything other than a relative process. Naturally, the conclusions arrived at by thinking may be either objective or subjective.

By refusing to admit ideals such as objective reality into its thinking, a mulehead confines itself to the relative world. That time bound underworld has its own set of doctrines. One of them is that the relative world (if it is not only an illusion) is the only one that exists. Perhaps, its most cherished doctrine is that there are no absolutes. Aside from the fact that, on the muleface of it that statement is oxymoronic, if there are no absolutes it cannot be an absolute certainty that the relative world is the only one that exists. Being pragmatists, muleheads are not terribly concerned by oxymoronic inconsistencies.

There is no doubt that in the New Age the doctrine of relativity is in the ascendancy, so the question arises, as far as the doctrine of absolutes, and the doctrine of relativity are concerned: which one is relevant? But, just because it arises does not mean it will be answered correctly; because, with the ascendancy of the superior court, (as opposed to the supreme court), a stroke of the pen is all that is necessary to turn that which is purely relevant into that which is purely irrelevant. Be that as it may, for purposes of discussion, this discourse, as much as logic and commonsense permits, will defer to that court's rulings.

Everything that occupies space is relative to everything else that occupies space. That's not a theory… just commonsense. When things are relevant to each other, their standards are relative to each other, as well. "Miles per hour" is not relevant to temperature, but is relevant to both turtles and speeding bullets. Where a speedometer, a thermometer, or any other "meter" is the standard, the measure is all a matter of degree. Time has to be among the most universal tools of measure. The face of the clock is the same all over the world, but even time is relative.

If midnight is the appointed hour, and clock 1 reads 11:59, while clock 2 reads 11:49, besides the ten minute difference, the thing that is most obvious, since they are approaching midnight at the same speed, is that the closer they come to it, the less relativity there is between the minute hand and the stroke of midnight. At zero degrees of difference, both relativity and approach vanish together. That alignment would seem to denote temporal perfection, except that clock 2 does not agree. In the absence of an objective standard, such as an atomic clock, which clock is correct becomes a matter of opinion, and the time is relative again. The supporters of clock 1, for their own reasons, have their "own time"; and the supporters of clock 2 have their "own time", for their own reasons. Not a problem, the issue is soon resolved because both groups have been superbly indoctrinated, inundated, and baptized, in the virtue of tolerance. Without going through a long de-rigmaroling process, it would be difficult to challenge the assertion that it was the relativity that is innate in tolerance that saved the midnight.

Both clocks could be wrong. One could be wrong, and the other could be right; but it is a leadbat cinch that both cannot be right about that particular midnight...unless the doctrine of tolerance is brought to bear. At the time that tolerance is brought to bear, it stands out in bold relief as its own best witness against its own stand (6 o'clock low)... which is diametrically opposed to the objective reality, (12:o'clock high). Naturally, when the doctrine of "own truth" – yours – mine – his – hers – theirs – ours – anybody's – is brought to bear, there is bound to be some confusion – like when all the traffic lights at an intersection are stuck on green. But, where muleheads are concerned, confusion is the name of the game. So, when traffic is snarled, and there are fender benders, and road rage, and collateral damage, and such things; — well, that is all in the game.

Naturally, when the supernatural standard... objective reality, has been punted clean out of the stadium, and the dome sealed, relativity seems to be the only game in town. When relativity is king, and all have their "own truth", and all have tolerance (especially for muleheads who gave them their truths), muleheads and the superior courts they use to validate and certify their unseemly seam-antics abound. When muleheads abound, confusion mushrooms, and out of its reign, now blatant in its boldness, evolution ensues and proceeds to ooze like radio-active, airwave-borne, putrefaction. So, the question: "Does anyone really know what time it is?" begins to become as salient in its poignancy as it was intended to be when it was barely able to rise above a whisper before being quenched by the sound of silence. Not to worry – the sun knows what time it is, and so do all of its shadows.

The upshot is that the acts which enthrone the actuality of relativity as the sine qua non of relevance do not interface with the standard set by reality. The downfall is that those acts mean no more to reality than a spider web on an aircraft carrier (trying to be an aircraft catcher in the brine) means to a landing F-16. When that spider web catches that F-16, it will have proved that it is relevant. Until it does; that evolutionary potty-pottage force fed to innocents at the training tables of the global village has become every bit as irrelevant as the logical upswing at the end of the sound of a supernatural silence that has, suddenly, become quite relevant.

XXXXXXXXXX

BEING presupposes life, power, and will. Will presupposes thought, consciousness, and intelligence. The very presence of existance not only presupposes a means of expressing it into reality, but also presupposes that truth is intrinsic in the ethereal WORD which is the only possible means of accomplishing that deed. To deny that BEING is all of the above requires consciousness, will, choice, and the words to do so; but those requirements are all by-products of, and dependent upon, BEING. Thus, the presence of consciousness denies the intellect any logical ground to stand on in any attempt to launch a denial. At the same time, even against its will, the intellect confirms the fact that, in order to even think about BEING not being the The Ubiquitous Imperative, BEING, absolutely, is an imperative. So, alone, the thought of denying that all of the above are a given presupposes that all of the above are a given. Moreover, it does not take a lot of thought to see that that given is both irrefutable and uncontestable, which, in effect, means that it is beyond debate.

Be that as it may, no self-esteem respecting member of a scoffing species of mulehead elite can be pleased at having to face up to the overwhelming evidence that an issue it does not wish to agree with can even be thought of as being beyond debate. It just galls its craw that any proposition can come that close to agreement with the prophetic dictum that every knee shall bow and every tongue shall confess. And, to make matters worse, The Mulehead was quick to see that there was hardly any room for any semantical shenanigans at all. There was just barely enough room for it to turn its face to the wall while mumbling through clenched teeth (though supposedly playing possum) that idle speculations about pie-in-the-sky concepts that are impossible to take into the lab and subject to scientifically verifiable experimentation (that is observable and repeatable) are just a cloud nine refuge of the defeated. The whole proposition was just a waste of time with zero chance of ever evolving into anything substantial.

Yet, nothing is more observable and repeatable than the failure of muleheads to evolve a method of ignoring evidence without tacitly admitting, (as evidenced by studiously contemptuous sneers), that there is evidence to be ignored. Observably and repeatedly, they have failed to come up with an antidote for the malady that causes teeth to be clenched so tightly that, without any experimentation, it is easy to see that at least one set of mulehead jaws have become locked.

(Incidentally, there are scientific instruments calibrated to precisely measure the foot pounds of pressure generated by molar grinding.)

So, it is without fear of rebuttal that it can be said that BEING is its own repeatable and observable defense – or offense – depending on which way a "lockjaw" would like for his fossilized cookies to be crumbled. Chalk up one more in the logbook for that which is logical, and order that which is scatological to do a few archaeopteryx-style "buck and wing"s as it scats its way off the global stage and wings its way down into the black hole of faith in that which is unbelievable.

Belief in things not seen is faith. Faith in things that may, or may not, seem reasonable is religion. Faith in a theory that has no basis for belief, (other than evidence which has been slanted, twisted, and bent into a plethora of "posterized" hoaxes and frauds; — not to mention that evidence which has been ignored, withheld, and hidden… all in the name of the Machiavellian style pseudoscientific pragmatism that is supposed to ensure the "survival of the fittest"), is evolution.

To have faith in that primordial slime clot of a secular religion, which chanced to punch-in on a bogus time clock set to alarm for a generation of vipers, and, then, to disappear in a big slimy bang of primordial self-refutation, is to have faith in what, on the face of it, is a dead-in-the-water set of inordinate suppositions that, (since they cannot jibe with intrinsic presuppositions), are the salty, secular, pillars of an illogical bunch of religious jive that can't help but be just as slimy on its butt as it is on its mulehead face.

Believing that slime is bad enough, but foisting it off as education on captive audiences in cornered markets is so far beyond criminal it borders on the diabolical. The foisters' primary pragmatic doctrine seems to hinge on an abiding faith in their ability to slime on the body politic most of the time, and on the vast majority of the global student body (K through Phd) almost at will. Calling that crap a low down dirty trick is a compliment. The dirt they have already done is nothing compared to what they have on the think tank drawing boards – such as reducing the populations of the global village to what they consider to be optimum levels "by any means necessary," up to and including weapons of mass destruction. Without resorting to the poolhall jargon The Commoner would use, suffice it to say that those foisters are the scribes for a demon inspired conspiracy to propagandize the hoi polloi until they are tenderized enough to be cinderized enough to be efficiently ruled by a bunch of highly illumined, New Age, Baal worshipping, covert, old-world, coven clubs.

By logical extension, the whole so called education system of prevaricating foolishness perpetrated by that ilk owes a public apology to all who have, by an assortment of internecine hooks and crooks, been coerced into matriculating in curriculums clandestinely designed to take a stab at deifying that ilk's version of the brave new space-age, globally positioned, missile-riding, witchcraft. A class action suit might redress some of the grievousness... if the global superior courts didn't have to be included in the adverse action as co-defendants.

The fact that BEING stands revealed for what it was before the invention of time, (an incontestable immutable absolute), cannot help but throw a monkey wrench (call it loosey) into the theory of evolution's charade parade. Another way to put it, since evolution operates on a series of lies, is that the theory is a serial liar. Lies number one and two are that the theory denies that there is anything metaphysical about physical beginnings, and that defies logic because the lie, itself, is a metaphysical act; — and it's the genesis of evolution. In arithmetic terms, that is like kicking the zero and the number one out of the numerical lineup, and then declaring that, henceforth, the number two will take the place of the number one. The zero, being nothing, never existed as anything other than a figment of the imagination. By fiat, the metaphysical realm is ruled "scientifically" out of bounds.

This bit of self-deception is then written into the global curriculum, where it becomes a canon of academic law which is taught as fact, and, as such, it becomes a criteria for the grading of global village students. A by-law of that law is that all mental activity is simply a by-product of the interaction between neural synapses in the brain. That way, a by-product of the deception, not only covers up the deception, but, should the cover-up ever be discovered, puts the blame on a neural misfire in a physical organ. Again, the metaphysical realm is circumvented.

The "scientific" curriculum-implant, since it cannot be taken into a lab and observed under a microscope, is treated as though it never happened... another lie to be linked into the series. That treatment is justified by invoking the "survival of the fittest" clause, which presupposes the addendum: "There are no absolutes". Then, that invocation is conveniently forgotten, and, conveniently, the forgetting, itself, is forgotten. So, all is calm on all brave new world order fronts. Though that is only a bare bones genealogy of how that theory was begotten, parading those bones in an academic setting, by statute, is grounds for sitting in jail for months...in our global village.

The re-discovery of the "absolute" which is both undeniable and undeniably metaphysical, is the monkey wrench that loosens the nut and frees the domino theory to play its part in causing the theory of evolution to recoil. With the reemergence of the metaphysical floodlight from behind the manufactured clouds, comes the idea that, in light of the new light, perhaps the physical bones ought to be reexamined. After all, reemergence and reexamination seem to be semantically and logically related in some way. In light of the new light, not only Lucy's bones, but those of Nebraska man, and Piltdown man, and the ten foot tall skeletons of giants, who left footprints in stone to show they walked the land, which are kept hidden in global village museum basements, should all be reexamined. And the posters of foetal progression toward birth, along with the posterized missing links, should not be left out of the new light. And, if the new light is the cause of the domino theory causing the theory of evolution to uncoil, well that's the way it is when the light demanded by logic is applied to the data surrendered by bare bones. As The Commoner is fond of saying to his poolhall buddies, "That's the way the cookie crumbles." The scientific outlook inherent in that colloquialism is not different from the attitude that should be taken toward the bones.

This is not to say "dem bones gon walk around", but, then again, neither is it to say they won't. However that may be, without taking a step, they do speak volumes by yielding digits to do their talking. One thing they say is that, while the metaphysical lie cannot be seen under the microscope, any truth in the physical bones can... if they all don't, somehow, mysteriously, disappear from the basements of the museums of the global village. But even if they do, the geological juxtapositioning of Mt. St. Helens with the Grand Canyon will tell the same story. So it would seem that, whether or not "dem bones" walk around, "dem" stones "gon" cry out. Neither the mini canyon at Mt. St. Helens nor the Grand Canyon is likely to, mysteriously, disappear.

What the bones, stones, mountain, and canyon, all say, in no uncertain terms, is that the covens of "scientific" warlocks and witches, whose bread and brew depends on alluding to the metaphysical as a figment of the imagination and existance as an illusion, would do well to take another look at the nature of the logic involved in the milking of an illusion for their bread and brew. In light of the illness intrinsic in that logic, alluding to truth as relative, and alluding to BEING as inconsequential, should become so obviously ridiculous that those covens, seeing the handwriting on the wall (coven rhymes with oven), would also see that it would be wise to arrange to collect their pensions and move on toward, hopefully, regaining some semblance of mental equilibrium by making themselves a promise to, from now on, allude to nothing.

Highly esteemed transcendental theorist and gurus of both the Eastern and Western persuasions, having made a name for themselves (and a ton of money), since they are one in having miserably failed to transcend BEING; — in order to continue to be highly esteemed, must now transcend the urge to set transcendental policy and become extremely quiet. Without exception, all the highly intellectual scoffers who feel compelled to deny the existence of any absolutes; — in order to demonstrate that a modicum of their intellectual power remains in tact, must now, tactfully, be quiet, absolutely.

And it won't be a matter of gag rule, either. The whole lot of what remains after the sighting of the virus in the logic, and the mulehead refusal to see anything other than another pragmatic opportunity in the virulence, will be free as a breeze to scream like stuck hogs to the high heavens – oops, inappropriate terminology – scream to a variety of strata in the geologic column at the curtailment of their freedom for opportunism. Their failure to shut up will mean that they have succeeded at climbing into harm's way. In its slow roll, the boomerang continues to come about. Or maybe the drum roll is over. It could be that when Mt. St. Helens blew its stack in washing tons of geological flood-denying "BS" down into Spirit Lake, that was the pop of the starter's gun, and a coded signal to the saints to get ready to march because the "sweet chariot" was on its way to see to it that their mountain of humanistic hell ends.

At any rate of speed, what is destined to be overwhelmed, kicked to the curb, and inundated, are the fossil falsifications, the pseudoscientific jawboning obfuscation, the textbook fabrication, and all other brainsliming techniques calculated and designed for the deliberate miseducation of the global mind. The sound of howling will be one sign that the chariot is swinging sub-basements low. The net effect of all the resulting foul howling will be of non-effect, and will, in effect, amount to no more than a zero-sum diatribe by a whole dying tribe of low-balling IQ high priests... a bunch of nothings' ado about much they had hoped to keep hidden from the masses being groomed by outcome based three r's adulteration and the other – all the other – scholastic junk jiving masses of kids into being brave new world order asses addicted to the hedonistic dictum: "If it feels good, do it." Providentially, the boomerang knows those kids don't know what they are doing -- just like it knows everything else.

The progress made in the last generation toward total separation of the child from the family has been remarkably successful. The wedge between them is firmly in place, and now the screws just have to be judiciously tightened. The inference to be drawn is that there are congratulations all around the backrooms of the hijacked schoolboards that implement the policy sent down from on think tank high.

It is true that school systems are more than carcasses for voracious taxing bodies and political patronage parties, but not a great deal more. Classical education is no longer even an afterthought, not only because few New Age instructors know what it means, but also, because, in the new age agenda, public literacy is a hindrance to the survival of those who have deemed themselves most fit to survive. The malignant permissiveness brought about by the strategic, progressive, application of prescribed benign neglect is not discouraged so that after the shambles the cream of the crop can be remanufactured to New Age specifications; and the "gremlins at the picture show" crowd, with the help of mega doses of bad press, can gradually be pushed out to a dumping ground where it is most convenient for the devil to get at the hindmost.

Feigned official concern for the psyches of tykes is really a psychic raid on their (for the most part) unsuspecting little minds. The express (but covert) purpose of the psychic rape, designed by psychic programmers, is to increase the tolerance levels of little tummies to the point where Post

Modern dogma, such as "there are no absolutes," and related issues, such as "two mommies or two daddies are just as good as one of each", will be tolerated without an undue amount of regurgitation. Intuitive hard-wiring, reinforced by home training (competing with television and other electronic bilge outlets) is systematically shorted out by, sometimes smuggled-in, smutty, resource material used in what is euphemistically referred to as diversity training.

What used to be considered private matters, or matters of decency, are replaced by the prescribed degrees of Pavlovian style behavior-modifying kiddy pre-porn that is shunted-in to stand in the neural gap pryed apart for the measured introduction of warm fuzzy acceptance of both male and female (and other) versions of the role reversing sphincterism being instilled in little minds even as it is installed by superior courts as the normal, and, perhaps, when population control is factored into the pragmatic equation, preferred behavior. (That behavior may be warm and Ronald Mcdonald fuzzy in the school classroom, but it is a different flamboyant act when parading up and down Main Street.)

Speaking of dogma; that which is inherent in arithmetic computations is of secondary importance to teachers when the system-wide lesson plan's primary objective is to note and record how a kid <u>feels</u> about the success, or lack of same, on an exam... and then base the kid's grading on that feeling. Those recordings are reduced to digitized data and stored in a computer to be used as the reference points for when it is deemed desirable that a kiddy feel another, more malleable, way. At one time, the subterfuge was thinly disguised as educational altruism: now that it has its puppet strings attached, it is an "in your face" prying of kiddys away from their families. The goal is to make a present of the crop to the "switch" doctors of the global village who will determine which strata of a "scientifically" designed social wheel a brave new cookie cutter cog is supposed to fit into.

Keeping in mind, that, according to pragmatic studies, populations are already several hundred percent too high, the brilliance of the engineering of the lock step hip-hopping marches into the quagmire of existential degeneracy cannot be denied. The evidence of that expertise is the armies of headphoned hedonists bound by dope and gagged by heads full of the rap sheet music whose collateral damage is the do-it-yourself corp of dummies finger-popping its way into the concert corrals that are stationed along the way to the holding pens within hip-hopping distance of the altars built to make sacrifice to the New Age Baal. The authors of this confusion-with-an-agenda are the intellectual and ecclesiastical schizophrenic cyclops licensed and mandated by global village chieftains to commit what amounts to academic and doctrinal decapitations.

Schizophrenia would have to be a prerequisite for cultivating the tunnel vision necessary to avoid seeing the T-rex sized bites being ripped out of what is left of the pseudo-scientific foundations of the religion of evolution... even as the illogic of its philosophic pretensions are being ripped to shreds and eaten alive. The self-proclaimed flagship of the "scientific method" has become the leaky rowboat (call it Loosey) pursued by the "scientific method." The once avid hunter of missing links, spoiling for a debate, has become the spoil. Now, it can't be hunted down to be invited to engage in a debate… televised or otherwise. (If it could be found, the network would either feign technical difficulties or snatch the spectacle of a debacle off the air.)

One of the best kept science-related secrets of all time (read cover-up), which puts the "flat earth" public relations people to shame, is that evolution is still being touted in global village classrooms and media outlets as an aircraft carrier that has just retrieved a spaceship newly returned from discovering life on Mars, when even the available evidence supports the contention that it is more like a dead-in-the-water submerged submarine without a working periscope. If the hidden (by muleheads) evidence were made available, the sub would be more like a ghost rowboat so full of holes it wouldn't stand a ghost of a chance of outrunning even Noah's ark.

And even before all the chicanery that has been done has been shown-up for what it is, the schizoid cyclops will have begun to see that evolution is a "by any means necessary" excuse for turning global school systems into farm systems for the Post Modern foolishness giving rise to institutions dedicated to psychic pedagogic pedophilia. With sight will come encroaching sanity and ears to hear the bumper music heralding the advance of the cosmic boomerang. But just because the jig is up does not mean that the mulehead, with the dead albatross hanging around its neck, will not find some hooves to stick in its ears, and, with jaws locked, continue to go right on pretending to be playing-possum… all the while trying to figure out a way to get around the existance of an absolute.

XXXXXXXXXXX

The mulehead was so sick of the sound of the word absolute that it could not help interrupting its possum playing. Raising its head and pretending to be talking in its sleep, it mumbled, loud enough to be understood, that it had been misquoted. Moral! Moral! What it had said was that there are no <u>moral</u> absolutes. That simulation of a groggy interjection was, of course, a subterfuge leading to the installation of "my own" morality and "your own" morality, which are sons of the same kind of perdition that got the mulehead included out in the first place. The truth is that morality is as firmly based in truth as logic is in the Logos – and there is no possum-playing mulehead in it.

How could there be? — Whatever is based in truth runs a logical course through existance that, eventually, finds its way back to truth – like an electrical circuit. Over time, that circuit becomes the self-evident commonsense that a mulehead abhors. The understanding of the simple way that logic works (regardless of the complexity of its workings) sounds the death knell for intellectual elitism, think-tank pragmatism, and the rest of the philosophical nonsense that amounts to little more than a mess of outcome based potty pottage. But, just because the death knell has sounded, does not necessarily mean that the mulehead won't roll over and transmigrate into a "not"-head. Anything to avoid having to face up to the fact that the logical extension of the absolute is into dogma.

Negative dogma for "not"-heads

The absolute is not negotiable.
BEING is not ephemeral
Truth is not relative.
The ideal is not ideas.
The intellect is not deity.
The creature is not the Creator.
Evolution is not evolving.
The above is not arguable.
What is left is not right.
A mulehead is a possum.

Dogmatic as it is, the truth looks more like the graphic cosmologies to be found on the next page.

COSMOLOGY OF THE
THEOLOGIC COLUMN

IHVH
(OMNIPOTENCE) OMNI SCIENCE (OMNIPRESENCE)
CON SCIENCE
PRE SCIENCE
SCIENCE

RELIGION
METAPHYSICAL *PHYSICAL*

COSMOLOGY OF THE
GEOLOGIC COLUMN

BIG BANG
Primoidial Soup
Rocks Date Fossils
Fossils Date Rocks
Lucian Hoaxes + Other Frauds
Evolution (extinct)

The difference between the scientific method… a process, and science… a body of knowledge, is the difference between the grapevine and the grape. Because the aim of this discourse is not to explore theological imperatives, but to follow where logic leads, the origins of the vineyard and related issues will be given short shrift. No attempt will be made to discover how Omniscience condescends to conscience in the imputation of logical order to the prescience which results in additions to the body of knowledge that, by definition, is science.

Until a hypothesis accrues all the evidence necessary to become evident, it is not knowledge, it is belief. Faith in beliefs rooted in opinion rather than in evidence is faith in faith; the same kind of circular reasoning that reasons that reason is the reason for reason. The accumulation of evidence should be scientific, and will be more or less religious. However, it must be kept in mind that religiousness can depart from the scientific method, and may lead to belief – to heartfelt belief – in confusion leading to blindness, such as is the case with muleheads and trumped-up evolution.

It is the controlled, experimental, repeated, application of logic, with religiousness scrupulously governed by a scientific template, that builds a reliable ladder, rung by rung, to knowledge. (The understanding of that knowledge is a separate issue.)

Until that ladder is firmly in place, both top and bottom, belief in it is, at best, well founded faith, and, at worse, just a matter of opinion. The might, weight, or clout to declare an opinion to be taught as fact, by fiat, is decidedly unscientific. As the seed of the grape returns to the ground and grows another vine which produces more grapes, so it is with logic returning to the Logos. The upshot is that religion, good or ill, is merely the vine, and not the grape. As such, it is the footstool before the throne of science.

Again, because the intent of this discourse is not theological, but logical, the question of why men of the pulpit, who are in a direct logical and semantical line with OMNISCIENCE, and, therefore, are scientists; and the men in the lab coats, religiously seeking answers, and, therefore, are religionists, do not recognize the fact that their job descriptions are an inversion of both logical order and reality, will not be addressed. Instead, it will be noted, in passing, that a battle between creation and science is a logical absurdity because, together, they are the math that is the property of BEING, and battles are only possible within the confines of the bubble of existance... among the physical and metaphysical activities that abound in what can only be accurately represented as the aftermath of the math. After all, all over the universe the musical scales were set and in place before ever any earthly music was made. Accordingly, science is above the after-mathematical fray that is to be resolved with the return of the restorative powers inherent in the logic of the boomerang coming to destroy and devour illogic in one fell swoop... thereby relieving the groaning of a violated creation.

XXXXXX

Before going on to sum up, it is worth noting that the arrival of the telescope brought about the demise of the idea that the earth was the center of the solar system. While the arrival of the electron microscope does no harm to that well founded correction, it so thoroughly demolishes the idea of life evolving from a "simple" cell that a very interesting question is raised. As it turns out, the "simple" cell was seen to be a micro-mini marvel of symbiotic precision so complex that it makes the most advanced microchip look feeble enough to cause deep despair in Post Modern Humanistic ranks. Each cell is a tiny city, so perfectly self-contained that, if any one of its millions of functions goes awry that cell cannot live. It is so perfect, from inception, that it cannot evolve because there is no next level to attain to. The only possible thing it can do is mutate; — and that is just the opposite of evolution. So, the question raised is whether man might not be just as colossal to the tiny micro-universe as he is tiny to the macro-universe. In that hypothetical scenario, it is conceivable that man might be the logical center, not of the solar system, but of the universe itself. However that may be, BEING remains just as undisturbed as ever, and just as absolute as it is undisturbed.

A corollary of that observation is, if BEING is an absolute, the other side of the coin is that non-BEING has to be equally as absolute. (Non-BEING can exist as actuality with no basis in reality: — like "not"-heads and evolution). Indeed, actuality that is not already in BEING may crossover into BEING; but, since the mechanism for doing so is absolute truth, the absolute is not violated. It is the actuality that must relinquish its illogic. Non-BEING, under the proper conditions, may enter into BEING; but the reverse is not possible. BEING abhors a lie even more than nature abhors a vacuum. A lie can be turned into truth, but truth cannot be turned into a lie. It can only be perverted.

Accordingly, the doctrines of transmigration and reincarnation (as opposed to transfiguration) are in just as much trouble as evolution. Essentially, they are horizontal versions of that theory. If either transmigration or reincarnation could exist at all, it would have to be as a temporal aberration locked into the non-BEING that is destined for the abyss – like the demons that entered into the pigs. More likely, no different from the theory, they are like ladders with no reasonable place to rest either end. The theory has the Big Bang for either its pillow or footstool – depending on which end is the head of a tale whose primordial feats smell like the worst of the dickens. Those doctrines, being Eastern in origin, probably have their deluded headwaters in the world of illusion.

Speaking of evolution, which, by now, obviously is a euphemism for ignorance “gone to seed”; — if, for the sake of argument, BEING were canceled completely out of the equation, the theory would still amount to no more than a big blank. It’s preposterous. In other words, “after” would have to precede “before” in order for evolution to get out of the primordial pool. Naturally, that turns the universe inside out. So, it would have to follow, with the universe turned inside out, that there is no such thing as BEING. That’s how it would have to be in order for evolution to be a fact. That would mean that this page and all those that preceded it would have to be blank. If that is the case, then, evolution, with the aid of “millions and millions of years”, might have a chance (somewhere between zero and none) to evolve.

However, keeping in mind that evolution and BEING are mutually exclusive, if there is so much as a single jot, or a single tittle, on this page, or any that preceded it; then, logic says that it is evolution that has to be blank. (If all those pages were blank, it would be very fortunate for muleheads because they wouldn't have anything to refute. As a matter of fact, without evolution, there could be no such thing as a mulehead evolutionist.) But, if these pages are not blank, the best evolution can be is a Big Bang wannabe that just happens to be not one jot or tittle more than a big blank. Moreover, even for the sake of illogical argument, it is preposterous to even attempt to cancel BEING out of the equation because no cancellation is possible without presupposing the BEING that is supposed to be being canceled out for the sake of argument. Thus, it would appear that, either logically or illogically, evolution, as foisted, is, totally, a blank. Blank, blank, blank, and blank… three regulation strikes, and one for the sake of argument: evolution, without any doubt, is out. The mulehead will, of course, reserve the right to harbor "his own" doubt.

Although there cannot be even "his own" kind of doubt that the theory is a blankety-blank dog, the mulehead will not admit it. (Possibly, that is out of loyalty to the cult of mule-headism.) Despite being an animal lover – the kind that will get down on one knee to be licked in the face by dogs – logic cannot abide either a hypocritical mulehead or its hypothetically blank dog of a theory. Whenever it passes them (it does not linger.), it symbolically kicks the hypothetically pathetic dog in its blank, and proceeds, without stopping and without having to utter a word, to remind the mulehead of the pathogenetic origins of its evolutionary theory.

The original idea was pirated from the term "tree of life"; — which was retooled into the term "water of life". That concept was reconfigured into a primordial pool… bearing life in an "inside out" version of how a tree bears its fruit. Ta dahhh! By "might makes right", pragmatic, fiat, that ancient pool (millions and millions of years old) was declared to be the headwaters that harbored the "simple", life-bearing, cell, which, over millions and millions of years, evolved the few fittest to survive to reach the top of the food chain and become the crowning glory of the brave new, most high, Humanistic Universe.

The only thing necessary to scientifically confirm the theory of having been anointed by mother universe to be her husband was a transitional fossil linking lower forms of animals to the glorious evolution of those found fit to be deemed most high. Once that missing link was found, the whole human race could then, more comfortably, begin to act like animals; and they (muleheads), the most predatory, the heavy hitters, could take their anointed place in the batting order and step up to the plate (swept clean) reserved for the top dog collective. With the "simple" cell already safely ensconced in global village textbooks, if no missing link could be found, a dozen or so could (in this high-tech day and age) most certainly be manufactured.

However, with the evolution of primitive optics to high-tech instruments like the electron microscope, the concept of the "simple" cell, under the higher power, had to be greatly expanded. The concept had to be enlarged to make room for a microscopic sized system of interacting, interdependent, tiny machines, symbiotically locked into the simultaneous start-up time that allows zero time for evolving to complexity that is beyond belief (even while looking through the instrument at complexity that surpasses that of the solar system), but has to be believed.

Rolling right along toward proving evolution's "next level" point... technology, along with geology and archeology, rolls right along proving that the possum-playing mulehead has good reason to play possum. Instead of finding the "simple" cell that proves the mulehead is all-wise, the "scoping" finds trillions of billions of little machines (in just one pool) that all say otherwise. Just one "ha"! from each machine in just one of the tiny cells in the primordial pool would suffice to account for the peals of laughter at a theory that thinks all it has to do to get over is, by design, to "find" a few good missing links. Obviously, the theory is a blank; and it is just as obvious that the only way for it to continue to be is to continue to be a blank.

If a missing link were ever found – a nice sized one – it would have to be amused at the fact that, apparently, its finders would not have bothered to look at the fact that it had to be made up of cells. Even if the newly found link were not a hoax or a fraud, under the glare of the electrons, its cells would still have to tell a story that is identical with that of the godzillions of cells that never missed a single second of a single day on the linking job. Just like the story of the godzillions, the story of the cells in the missing link would overwhelmingly contradict the "millions and millions of years" of the mythological tales poured into the pryed apart seams of the text in science books.

It ought to go without saying that, in order for a link to truly be missing, it would have to be missing on the molecular level as well as on the cellular level. But lo! – even in the missing links – Hail, hail, the cells are all here… the possible exception to their perfect attendance might be the cancer cell. But cancer is a mutant that either mutes its host, or is muted quickly enough for any questions about its contributions to any missing linkage that is "millions and millions of years" old to be questions that are moot.

The predicament that both the theory of evolution and its promoters find themselves in is definitely not too funny to be put into words; — but why waste them? That would be overkill. The abundance of their own pseudoscientific words, amply recorded in chapters of global textbooks, is far more than enough to transmigrate those contaminated sections into the Post Modern comic books implanted right there between legitimate textbook covers. Those mythological tales should still be good for a chuckle or two even after being laughed at by kindergartners for "millions and millions of years". Right now, as they stand (read lie), they are a howl.

Having been discredited as science, evolution may redouble its efforts to salvage a place for itself by a media blitz to spin doctor its way into acceptance as a legitimate course of philosophic study. In that case, instead of moving on up to a deluxe cubicle in an ivory tower, it would be moving on up from a sub-basement to a cellar if it had its bearings. But, since science is on a plane higher than that of philosophy, and since the philosophy of pragmatism has its bearings inverted, what it would expect to be a climb up the ladder would turn out to be a boring expedition deeper down into a pitiful hole. Considering that its pragmatic underpinnings have preceded it, that is a boring act it shouldn't find too hard to follow.

An intellectual effort worthy of being called a philosophical endeavor is uncompromising in its quest to reach the solution that is ideal. Intellectual scheming that has wormed its way into philosophical circles is the perdition in disguise which gives the discipline a bad image. (Does not consort with any sense that is too common.) Disguised as a philosophy, the scheme undergirding evolution's efforts to gain respectability for its "scientific" crimes seems to be the one that sees history as a blending of thesis with antithesis to arrive at a synthesis. That synthesis then becomes the new thesis awaiting an antithesis so that it can leapfrog its way into the middle of the nest of the next generation of vipers.

Between leaps, deals are cut with any ally willing, by any means necessary, to do whatever it takes to advance the brave new world order agenda. So, the synthetic underpinning that purports to be forging its way toward a humanistic utopia, being without bearings, is really just a philosophical forgery boring its way back down into the pit from which the ancient model for the duplicitous construct came. It is only fitting that the dark-of-the-world, "in your face", theory of evolution should follow that counterfeit.

Unlike with synthetic pretenders whose principal aim seems to be to leave behind a legacy of more sophisticated questions and an impressive bibliography, the truly philosophical endeavor eventually rises to a point where it is included in the body of knowledge that has proved to be science. Led by logic, the activity of the search ceases as the quest comes to rest under the shadow of OMNISCIENCE. Unavoidably, logic... the mailman... has delivered the philosophical package to the correct address and deposited it on the doorstep of the mansion of theology; because, logically, that's where it belongs. Since logic and the Word are inextricably bound, logic's round trip back to the Logos is also a returning of the Word to the Father. In doing so, it completes another closing of the singular circuit (beyond the reach of synthetic short circuits) that gives light to the world. Viewed from another perspective, the fact that there is any light left in a world duped into believing that it is evolving is proof positive that the true Word cannot have returned from his tour of duty as the son of man void.

So, there will be no evolving into a brave new transcendentally humanistic Post Modern nirvana of a utopian world order. (It would only be a Post Modern continuation of the same old humanistic disorder.) The same order that was already preset from the beginning is the one, defanged and debugged, that has already been reset (at the cross) to be restored at the end. As it is in the scientific realm, so it is in the philosophic domain; for evolution, being without BEING, there just is no room in the inn.

But just because there is no room does not mean that, after all is said and done, the mulehead is finished. On the way to the manger out back, it is still scheming. It is not generally realized just how slick a mulehead can be. Even if it were generally realized, it would not be generally believed. Normalcy just cannot believe that even a mulehead would duct tape its eyes and ears so that the polygraph would support its contention that it has neither seen nor heard any evidence against evolution. When it comes to the survival of the "fittest", the various scopes (micro and macro) of its self-deluding spin doctoring abilities are legendary.

And it could be that the whole evolution-foisting is just a diversionary tactic... a smokescreen to hide the mule-head's more sinister motive; — like the setting up of its itty-bitty cohorts, who think they have been found most fit to survive, for total annihilation. There can be no doubt that the promotion of the theory of evolution is only one symptom of a problem that goes much deeper than geo-political con games. Perhaps, the mulehead is just being loyal to its big brother, or maybe it is suffering from the same congenital defect... rebellion. Or, perhaps, in its ambition, the mule-head secretly wishes to co-host the rebellion. The question is whether a possum-playing mulehead is knuckleheaded enough to allow itself to be a deadhead already destined to be a "not"-head, or is it still heady enough to exercise its choice between being included in and being included out. There are those who think that it is a gigantic mistake for muleheads to even have a choice. They think its inalienable right to choice should be rescinded. Ironically, that is the same stuff of which choice-usurping muleheads are made.

XXXXXXXXXX

To sum up: with or without deadheads, the word is alive. It is alive in the sense that an electrical wire or an energized battery is alive. The difference is that the word cannot die. The truth intrinsic in the melding of thought with its symbolic alphabetical representation means that life, word, and truth are synomous terms. (Animated existance is not necessarily life.) The fact that thought is conveyed by a symbol means that the word, if the truth is the light, is the light also. Since it is the way of the word to be a dispenser of light, it is the door to further light as well. Moreover, the word is a servant. Like a flock of sheep, herded words follow their shepherd wherever he wishes them to go. Viewed as obedient children, they are living proof that they are the son of man whose very existance proves that none of the above can be successfully disputed. The herd of words used in any attempted disputation, by their use, serve only to affirm that, even when obscured by clouds, the word is still the sun of man. That is another way of saying that the word is the light of the world.

The essence of the word is in the agreement between the symbol and that which has been symbolized. The seamlessness of that agreement is the living proof of the truth that forms its core. The radiance of the truth... intrinsic, inherent, and innate, is the rays of logic that are its substance. Just as a single brick cannot cause a wall to be crooked; obviously, because of the way that it comes to be, it is impossible for a word, in and of itself, to lie. Even when it has been semantically raped, robbed, and mugged, so that its meaning has been substantially altered, its truth, which is fundamental rather than elemental, remains, essentially, untouched. Though the body of its truth be crucified, the spirit of its truth remains to resurrect a body of truth even more fearfully and wonderfully made. After all, the life that goes into the composition of the word is eternal, and, therefore, cannot be extirpated.

The only logical inference is that life, which cannot be taken, has to be considered a given. A given, which presupposes a Giver, it would seem, should elicit at least a little bit of gratitude.

Yet, the word is taken as much for granted as the hard-wiring in the brain designed to receive and decode the symbols that carry its messages. No sooner has it been used to convey an idea than its contribution to the communication is micro-minimized; and it is treated as though it were a discarded candy bar wrapper. Even of those who know it, few bother to note that, as great as BEING is... The Ubiquitous Imperative, the universal singularity... there would be no way to know it if BEING, itself, whatever else it may be, were not also a word.

Just as thought presupposes a thinker, the word presupposes a speaker. The truth in that presupposition is the third side of the triangle in a triune pattern that echoes, — past, present, and future, throughout the whole, dust — to form– to dust, creation. The speaker (1), the word (2), and the truth (3) of the relationship, comprises the trinity of the Godhead. The reality of that trinity is not contestable without the trinity of thought, word, and deed (or misdeed) doing the contesting. It's a lock; the contesting is, itself, a trinity that cannot avoid affirming the reality of the trinity.

Like it, or lump it; — it is not possible to either like it, or lump it, without bowing the knee to the omni-presence of the triune pattern in the third dimension. Pointing out the fact that genuflection, voluntarily or involuntarily, is unavoidable, and always will be, simply reveals that a declaration was made about a preexisting order that was already a fact of life when the declaration was made. But the sight of men had already degenerated to a state of being unable to see through paradox. So, the prophetic utterance was not one that threatened torture until the knee was forced to bow, but a prediction that an age would come when blind eyes would be enabled to see the triune pattern which includes the very eyes needed to see that the knee is already bowed, and has been throughout all of time. Seeing that, there would be less of a problem seeing that the hard-wiring in the brain is also an integral part of the pattern. Any confessing, pro or con, that is going to be done, in any language, has to go through that wiring to come out as a tongue. That's just common-sense. Thought fathers the word that must give the order of a deed before any deed can be done. Involuntary orders, like heartbeats and such, were given by the ideal *WORD* before creation began. Being perfection itself, the *WORD* had no need to wait to evolve toward reaching a state where He already was…and still is.

The archetypal *WORD* is so close to being the ultimate reality that He is both the ideal and only way to approach reality. Neither is the only begotten *SON* the child of the *FATHER*…as men think of sons. Rather He is the expression of the power of the *FATHER*. Just as potency is, and always has been, one with omnipotence, the *WORD* is, and always has been, one with the *FATHER*. Since the truth of the accord of their relationship transcends, pervades, and encompasses time, there never can be a time when that accord is not truth… so much so that the *SPIRIT* of truth is an equal partner in that accord. The magnitude of that mystery is such that theologians, in a state of mental recoil on the border of cognitive dissonance, simply assign to an imponderable majesty the four letters (IHVH) they call the Tetragrammaton, and let it go at that. And some of them are not aware that is the *CHRIST*.

Though it may seem so to time bound thinking, the *CHRIST* is not a lower order than the *FATHER*. His true glory is tempered to avoid overwhelming creatures with the magnificence of an immutable absolute whose sudden revelation would most certainly cause mortal eyes to consume away on the same spot where mortal bodies fall into the faint that is not a spell, and from which there can be no awaking. So great would be the horror, upon becoming aware of the unbridgable chasm between what they are and what they were made to be, and the realization of who the *CHRIST* truly is, that their hearts would simply fail at the consciousness of the unbearableness of their own ugliness. The fact that the *CHRIST* is not seen does not mean that He is not here in the now. The veiling of his presence is an extension of his mercy. And, were it not for the silent workings of his sustaining spirit, the earth would now be no more than a malignant cinder. In the deed of earth-saving truth, the *FATHER*, the *SON*, and the *SPIRIT*, are one.

The flesh, like all things created, material and non-material, is a byword of the *WORD*. To the degree that an ordained trail of letters lays rails in a bed that is true to its orders, its direction will be trained on its preordained destination with truth in language. Language enters flesh to be amplified and come out enhanced for the next round of truth. In that way, the way is light lighting the way to more light, and, in doing so, language becomes an extension of the perfection of the light that is the Son of God. That extension of perfection is not different from it, but a magnification and proliferation of that from which it receives its direction. Thus, the flesh whose choice is to be directed by the *WORD* is a proliferating byword. The Creator and the ordained creature are as much one as any master of art and his masterpiece. Since the *WORD* is the Master of all masters, it's just commonsense that his masterpiece has to be the masterpiece of all masterpieces.

Before the plan left the drawing board, the death of the redeemer was deemed to be crucial if the logic in the mathematics of the pattern was to be preserved. A key element and carrier of the potential, either for the plan's proliferating growth, or for its demise, was choice. Under no circumstances could choice be violated without destroying the plan… utterly. Any abridgement of the freedom innate in choice would cancel all hope for any potential for growth. And the only way to be rid of the potential for death, inherent in the plan, was to allow that potential to be exercised.

Then, the penalty of death would have to be paid by one who is innocent of exercising that potential, or the exacting mathematics of the logical pattern, which calls for the annihilation of that which is no longer perfect, would be visited upon that imperfection… and that would be the death of the plan. Payment of the penalty by the innocent would not only exhaust the potential for death, but would also throw the logic of the mathematical pattern out of kilter. By killing the innocent, death violated truth, and, in doing so, became guilty of the logical inconsistency that left it out on a limb at the mercy of the prescribed flight pattern described by the correcting arc of the boomerang. Of course, the restoration of logical equilibrium to the mathematics of the pattern automatically meant the death sentence for death.

It was the incarnated *WORD* who entered fatally flawed time as the truth that had to be re-seeded in it. The truth is that submission to truth, all the way up to and including physical death, was the truth needed to repair the breech between logic and the Logos. That repair restored access to the sight to see the Grand Canyon-like stratum of lies clouding eyes to the fact that the truth, in and of itself, is as much the absolute of all absolutes as logic is the offspring of the Logos. That reparation restored access to the light needed to see that any springing off from belief in that absolute is just another blind, fruitless, excursion into the pigsty of illogic by another humanistically prodigal son. Not only is any resistance to absolute truth futile, it is impossible. Resistance requires the assistance of either logic or illogic, but neither is available because both are previously engaged, one positively and the other negatively, in assisting in the support of the irrefutable proof that the sovereignty of the Logos, either logically or illogically, is absolutely a given.

Therefore, resistance is not stillborn, and it is not aborted. It is not even conceived because conception is not possible without the assistance of the Logos. There is just no conceivable way of conceiving any resistance without an assist from the Logos, and that very assist can only serve to reiterate the fact that, without the Logos, there is no way for resistance to be conceived. To even expend the effort to try to bypass the inconceivable is an effort to reverse the forward momentum of the universe, and that, besides being a waste of effort, is an expenditure that is absurd and/or insane. So it would seem that the only option left for a would-be resister is the fruitless rebellion which would be just another vain exercise doomed to expire in a paroxysm of nothingness. It does not take a degree in rocket science to see that resistance without assistance is futile. That's just commonsense.

That sense is so common that it would be difficult for even a moron to miss sensing that the plan that was merely "very good" in the beginning, having exhausted its potential for prodigality, and having been tried and trued, is very beautiful in the end. Before the beginning, when all was perfection, it's just commonsense that excellence was superfluous. Perfection cannot be excelled. Now, after the fall, since there are no secrets… only mysteries awaiting further light; — on the rise, the sky will be, (and now is), the only limit.

Accordingly, however it must be spelled to accommodate any tongue, Jesus, the Christ, is the name synonymous with, and the logical equivalent of, both truth and the word. The *WORD* is the All in all enabled to see that the departure from the *FATHER* was by the Son of God who returned to the *FATHER* as the resurrected Son of man. At this juncture, it should be obvious that, without the word to provide the light, any thought of refutation is worth less than a blank in a blackout. Any attempt to deny the sovereignty of the WORD must bow to the word simply to access the power necessary to make any foredoomed attempt. By means of its ground, the earth brings forth its fruits to man. The brain is the ground for the word whose flowering is light to the world and whose spirit is a fragrance to God.

Of a truth, the only way to the *FATHER* is through the *SON*. The only alternative is to decline the invitation to the supper. When the last jot and tittle of the loggings in the logbook of the Logos is checked off, a circuit is closed. Gradually, the pattern of the logic in the plan begins to emerge; and understanding comes with the dawning of the light. The choice will be (and now is) between reflecting or deflecting that light. In either case, there will be a genuflection… a bowing in, or a bowing out. In either case, the last bow will be the signal for the myriad choirs to begin singing praises for the restoration of the sight to see that to mind meld with the Alpha and Omega is to join the circle glowing with the understanding of the one universal Son who, absolutely, is without peer.

Already, the incarnation, the crucifixion, and the resurrection are the beginning, middle, and end of the three day love song scored by Jesus (in three days) for the day when, as the Tetragrammation, he returns to wed the bride he claimed two millennia ago when he said: "It is finished".

STRING OF PEARLS

WORD

Between inner oceans, it names ships of thought
Set to sail wherever two thinkers agree they ought.
The letter of its law formed the mires
Its spirit transforms into graceful spires
Whose ringing bells in wedding reason with rhyme
Are wings as well, into eternity, outside all time.
It is means of gaining comforting calm
From that everlasting stream of healing balm
Whose current dissolves discord in the cosmic course
Echoing the Solo… itself an echo of the unnameable Source.

Nothing to see, smell, taste, hear, or feel:
Beyond ephemeral sensors is that ethereal
Elemental medium more elusive than air;
But, for rays to radiate, it has to be there.
The infinite, infinitesimal, aura of the immutable
Is beyond number, so numerically inscrutable.
Undivided at division into paradox,
Indivisible from revision of its equinox,
Equally present in every facet of all spacings,
And, facing all abouts; it is without abouts in facings.

ETHER

'M OTHER

Ethereal song, into the void, flows-forth…a vibrance.
A tune of One Tone surges-forth…its resonance.
In sequence, light bursts-forth: hence matter.
Consequently, to the void, comes shadow.
This separation—strewing swirling cosmic light
Into farthest reaches of that unfathomable night
Imagination must ponder to attempt to perceive,
And that, if birth is into light, has to be believed —
Is womb of all wombs…an ever-changing container.
Changeless indeed its Indwelling Sustainer.

UNIVERSE

With outpouring light, revolving forms begin evolving...
Reaching various heights, they begin dissolving.
Each evolving toward dissolving is a rhythm with a rhyme.
Rhythm's breadth, birth to death, is rhyme of its time.
From the spire of rhythm's pre-seeded crescendos, the cosmic way
Spirals re-seeding solos evolving rhymes that interplay.
As infinitesimal... atomically small and too many to count,
Is of the infinite... astronomically large and continuing to mount,
So are these solos, rhythmically bound and harmoniously interspersed,
Only primal echos resolved in the ethereal song of the universe.

COSMOS

From where a speck of cosmic dust per cubic-space-mile
Telescopes as light-years-long cloud-like isles
Suspended over yawning chasms of cosmic abyss,
Star pools are as clusters of whorl-shaped clouds of mist.
In a prepetual bond, though perpetually being freed,
Apparent stillness expands at such stupendous speed
Dimension itself seems out of the realm of the real.
Of such is the magnitude of galaxial wheels.
In ever-outflowing light-years, whirls each cosmic day:
Just a grain among the sands is the Milky way.

MILKY WAY

From within, galaxial form can only be seen
As tiny dots of stellar days sending twinkling beams
Across abysmally remote spans of space so vast
They gleam in the present from time that is past.
So the sun is star of its own show,
With a retinue of dwarfted planets orbiting in tow…
Endlessly warming their hemispheric faces
By everlasting trading of their hemispheric places.
Gargantuan is glare as its raw power comes unbound;
A behemoth beacon without a tower is asunder from all sundown.

SUN

Without haste, at a most gradual pace,
Does it assume ascendancy over nearer outer-space.
At times it is a luminous blue hole in velvet-night's tent…
Other times, in blue distance, a sliver of silver crescent.
But even overshadowed from the source of its shine,
As constant is its one face as — cyclical its times.
Misty beams it flings it neither has nor holds,
But over liquid rhythms it exerts the mystical control
That bids tides to ebb and looses oceans to flow.
Without fail, as it comes, does it go.

MOON

The basin of waters, food of fire,
Is fertility's fount, and hub of desire.
Here the Eternal comes to learn of age
On a rotating, transforming, perfecting stage.
Its soil is the womb of seeds that take root,
As well as the tomb of seeds' flower and fruit
Where Nature's tours and creatures meet in matter's rounds
Of elemental and fundamental circuits sharing common ground.
A globe, orbiting a star going its galactic way,
Faces universal night…follows a perpetual day.

EARTH

Choirs of clouds burst over valley and peak…
Pouring a drenching on mighty and meek…
Filling rills rushing in an endless wet train
Into rivers, removing, renewing, refacing, terrain.
Slightest downslope…downward its fluid motion
Till it pools, or rests in a roll of the ocean.
Given time, through hardest rock, it will bore.
Yet, as invisible mist does it soar
From its drainings to re-root in the gloom
Of perspiring choirs, poised, to resume.

WATER

To clouds…speed; to the breathing…life;
To sound…a steed; to velocity it is strife.
Lashed into blasts that are tortured into squalls,
The gale, howling beneath the low and above the tall,
Was a zephyr before such screams were born
Of the gusts, in deep calm, still forerunning such storms.
An everlasting envelope, the placenta of air,
First and last lodger in every earth lair,
Is unending in wendings sealed without a seam:
Yet, by no eye has it ever been seen.

AIR

Inert, behind the spark, heavy with yearning,
Weightless flame waits for baptism into burning.
Its tongues elude grasp, yet are painfully felt.
Its heat compels the melting to melt.
Unleashed, it is a blind inferno of blazing appetite
Able to torch high-noon out of blackest midnight…
Devouring trees until whole forests are gone.
It is what forces volcanos to vomit liquefied stone.
The revolving door of an energy-filled void,
Returns, innate, in rebirth of all its destroyed.

FIRE

Ice shards ring ponds… chill winds turn raw.
Freezing leaks form ice-daggers in a frigid jaw.
The snap in frigidity's bite locks even putrefaction.
In the rigid and tight lies winter's satisfaction.
Evergreens' arm-shadows become ever-colder caves
Remolded by blizzards between ever-colder waves.
Swirling, shrouding, clouds of powdery white
Crest, crust, and glare, from ever rising heights
Deepening suppression in growth's resting rhythms
Until, in succession, re-dawning green comes.

WINTER

Stronger rays relax rigidity in frigidity's jaw.
Longer stays and brighter tones begin the thaw.
Lengthening days are spring's sunny dawn:
The haze they raise is greening grasses' yawn.
Showy, towering, clouds gather and pour down showers
On meadows ballooning kaleidoscopic swarms of flowers.
Scurrying shadows of the fleecy fleet, sculling breezes
Teasing mushrooming billows of budding leaves,
Skim glossy grasses wafting continual visual songs.
In waves upon waves, the green comes.

SPRING

The glimpsed glaring halo too dazzling to behold
Leaves a blue-naveled after-image of the hottest, whitest, gold
That torches barren land into a broiling rack,
And scorches the small river up from its track
While giving energy to grow to green's multitude
Busy generating tissue without interlude.
Green's fruitful issue, issues-forth the seeds
Of greening's progressions… a proliferation indeed.
In many-hued flourishes, summer's cornucopic crescendos
Gush from their wellspring…its many green flows.

SUMMER

Gold's tone in rays deepens upon their loss of heat.
Autumn's yellow-advance is summer's green-retreat.
Mellowed petals fall before increasing cold.
Trees are as spired choirs of clouds of reds or rusts or gold.
Bulbous fruit plops. Leaves just rustle down...
Joining compacting compost rejoining the ground.
Through web-works of bare branches appears the skyline.
With decreasing degrees, color wanes, except in the Pine...
Ever green, and awaiting the snows.
Last is grass; then its sheen goes.

AUTUMN

Startling is the shock of Manifestations's birth,
For trauma trips the trapdoor onto relative earth
Bringing Like, so Dislike... twin faces of all desire.
Silence, is Like's repose. Rage, is Dislike's ire:
But cradled to breasts in its nest and new home,
The babe matches its smile with the one it owns.
Blinks of its eyes are branching-out of belief
That blossoms in returns of its missing chief.
Thus fruit of the womb born half wild
Gropes to see through eyes of a child.

BABE

To eyes able to mark a season's decline
Weaning is an ark up reasons's incline.
The straggler lifted from the tail
Grows giving lifts to toddlers who trail:
Learning form… figment congealed; color… pigment revealed,
Are both ephemeral spokes in Nature's re-creating wheel.
For the urge leading to uncommon desires,
The Common Sense knows the balance required
Is child-play so creative in style
As to multiply wonder in the eye of the child.

ASCENT

Pre-seeded by the Indwelling Doer of all deeds,
Seed-bearer and carrier mate and mother life's seed;
Thus, as fat swells through lean,
Life's ultimate end indwells it means.
In the course of duty, their tugs and shoves
Are life exercising the fidelity of its beloved.
So, male and female, are they groomed to understand
That all redound to the Sound of One Hand.
No matter the harvest, dutiful offsprings smile
For Milk of One Breast, with eyes of a child.

DOOR

WAY

Behind is one eternity; before is another:
Eternal is creation of the one from the other.
The Way gives way, first through last:
Only the un-fore-going remain mired in the past.
Behind, but not left behind, are these off the pace,
For eternally everlasting is the nature of the grace
Where rage, lust, and greed, doors to one tragedy,
Re-open at a knock to the Way of the One's majesty.
Echoing the sage, the toddler said: The sun never dies…
Manifestation resolves as Earth revolves; thus it appears to rise.

CHRIST

Manifestation strayed into time and its impairings.
Pre-ordained grace began its task of merciful repairings.
In time, into time, to restore a belief flown,
Descended the Son, careful to do no thing of His own.
Acknowledging the Father every step of the way,
He fashioned light of a darkness grown to think itself day.
As Paradise, by our Father, was the Earth deemed.
As Paradise, by the risen Son, was it re-deemed.
The shepherd of all toward life's one goal
Is gatherer of the many flocks into one fold.

JESUS

IHVH

Unchanging is the infinite sea of bliss that never began:
It is Truth, and beyond change, so never can end.
Supreme is the triune accord so serenely alone
That seers say, by seeking, may be fully known.
And they say: neither high nor low is this holy One,
But centered, in Manifestation, as in the sinless Son's
Submission of will to that consciousness absolutely pure…
Fount of self-luminous wisdom, peace, and love absolutely sure.
They further say: uncaused is the Source of the Begetter of all begot,
Being equally in and beyond what is, as well as is not.

FATHER

BEGINNING

The Godhead, too at one to create, wills the Creator
Of opposites and their stabilizing equator.
This Unmanifest Begetter fathers the idea Ideal.
In Lordly lineage, descends the Ultimate Reality into the real.
With the merely real comes unreality, the primal pair.
Being, thus not-being, the primal root, is there.
With the potentially unlovely, graciously, restored to loveliness,
This Flawless Conception issues-forth to manifest.
Ethereal Music to the Ethereal Ear is the Ethereal Word:
Universally, hearing hears—-as at first it universally heard.

Printed in the United States
216813BV00001B/1/P

9 781607 913504